Shakespeare's Globe Theater

Other titles in the *History's Great Structures* series include:

The Eiffel Tower

The Great Wall of China

The Medieval Castle

The Parthenon of Ancient Greece

The Roman Colosseum

The World Trade Center

History's Great STRUCTURES

Shakespeare's Globe Theater

David Robson

ReferencePoint Press®

San Diego, CA

© 2014 ReferencePoint Press, Inc.
Printed in the United States

For more information, contact:
ReferencePoint Press, Inc.
PO Box 27779
San Diego, CA 92198
www.ReferencePointPress.com

LIBRARY OF CONGRESS CATALOGING-IN-PUBLICATION DATA

Robson, David, 1966-
  Shakespeare's Globe Theater / by David Robson.
    pages cm. -- (History's Great Structures)
  Includes bibliographical references and index.
  ISBN-13: 978-1-60152-542-0 (hardback)
  ISBN-10: 1-60152-542-7 (hardback)
  1. Globe Theatre (London, England : 1599-1644)--Juvenile literature. 2. Shakespeare, William, 1564-1616--Juvenile literature. I. Title.
  PR2920.R63 2013
  792.09421'64--dc23
                                                              2012046061

CONTENTS

Important Events in the History of
Shakespeare's Globe Theater   6

Introduction   8
  Lost and Found

Chapter One   12
  Theater Before the Globe

Chapter Two   25
  Origins

Chapter Three   40
  Globe Heyday

Chapter Four   53
  Fire, Rebuilding, and Death

Chapter Five   67
  Globe for a Modern Age

Source Notes   81

Facts About Shakespeare's Globe Theater   85

For Further Research   87

Index   89

Picture Credits   95

About the Author   96

IMPORTANT EVENTS IN THE HISTORY OF SHAKESPEARE'S GLOBE THEATER

1598

Under cover of darkness, timber from The Theatre is taken for use in building a new theater, soon to be named the Globe. Shakespeare is mentioned as its "principal comedian," or main comedic actor.

1594

The Chamberlain's Men is formed, with William Shakespeare as primary playwright and Richard Burbage its most famous actor.

1613

In June, fire destroys the Globe theater.

1564

William Shakespeare is born in April in Stratford.

1587

An open-air theater, the Rose, is opened.

1550 1570 1590 1610

1576

The first commercial theater, named The Theatre, opens in Shoreditch, London.

1593

London's theaters close due to the bubonic plague.

1599

The Globe theater is opened in Bankside, London.

[The Globe Theatre, Bankside.]

1608

Richard Burbage takes back the lease for the Blackfriars theater. The King's Men, including Shakespeare, become part owners. The theater is used for winter performances.

1614
The Globe theater is rebuilt on its original foundations; the roof is tiled, not thatched.

1982
Professor John Orrell provides new evidence on the shape and dimensions of the Globe after analyzing a 1647 map of London by Wenceslas Hollar.

1642
The English Civil War breaks out between Puritans from parliament and Royalists, loyal to the king. Parliament suppresses all stage plays.

1997
The opening season of the newly rebuilt Shakespeare's Globe includes Shakespeare's *Henry V* and *The Winter's Tale*.

1817
German scholar Ludwig Tieck visits London, studies theater owner Philip Henslowe's papers, and wonders whether the Globe can be rebuilt.

1660
King Charles II is restored to the throne of England; theaters reopen.

1650   1775   1900   2025

1644
The Globe theater is demolished by the Puritans. It is replaced by tenements for London's poor.

1969
American actor Sam Wanamaker starts campaigns to rebuild the Globe theater in London.

1616
In April, Shakespeare dies and is buried in Holy Trinity Church in Stratford.

1991
Construction work begins on the foundations of the theater complex.

2012
Artistic director of Shakespeare's Globe announces plans to build a 340-seat, indoor theater space within the Globe complex to be opened in 2014.

Lost and Found

In 1596 Johannes De Witt, a Dutch tourist, entered the Swan theater in London. Once seated, he took out his notepad and sketched the interior of the playhouse. De Witt's rendering shows a view from high in the upper galleries of the Swan, looking down. Front and center is a wide stage upon which three actors perform. Behind them are two doors leading to the tiring-house, where the performers donned their costumes; above this are balconies and towerlike spaces. De Witt's sketch was eventually lost, but an unknown friend had made a copy, and nearly three hundred years later the modest but detailed drawing was discovered at the University of Utrecht in the Netherlands by a German historian named Karl Gaedertz. This sketch is the only existing illustration of the interior of a theater of that era. Without this copy of De Witt's drawing, contemporary scholars and theater lovers would likely have no concept of what early playhouses, including the Globe theater, one of history's great structures, looked like on the inside.

WORDS IN CONTEXT

tiring-house
Building located within an Elizabethan theater in which actors prepare and change costumes.

Little Is Known

Beyond the evidence provided by De Witt's drawing, little is known about sixteenth century theaters such as the Globe. Built in 1599, it was once but one of a handful of playhouses that dotted the city of London. These included the Curtain, the Rose, and Blackfriars, all of which competed to draw audiences by keeping their live entertainment fresh. New plays written by some of the brightest minds of the age were always in the offing; performers worked tirelessly to learn new lines of dialogue during the morning and evening hours for performances that took place in the afternoon.

To this day the Globe's exact physical dimensions are unknown. For years researchers believed the Globe was a round building, yet recent research has determined that it was actually a twenty-sided

In its heyday the Globe attracted a cross-section of London society with plays written by some of the brightest minds of the age. Although the theater succumbed to fire and other indignities, it has since been restored to its former glory.

polygon. Built of timber and plaster, with a roof made of thatch, or dried grass, it was a three-story structure and could hold up to three thousand people at one time.

During its heyday, the Globe welcomed all Londoners—rich and poor, gravedigger and duke. While its audiences represented a cross-section of London, most patrons paid a penny for admission. And in return the playhouses offered patrons a rich mix of plays. But, like other theaters of its time, it occasionally had to shutter its doors for fear of plague. And then—fourteen years after it was built—the Globe succumbed to fire. Although it was reconstructed, the Globe later closed again—this time by order of a puritanical British government.

Playwright's Theater

From these and other morsels of information, historians have also further excavated the Elizabethan age (named for Queen Elizabeth I, who ruled from 1558 to 1603) and, in particular, the life of the period's most acclaimed playwright, William Shakespeare. Born in rural England, Shakespeare married young, traveled to London, and quickly established himself as a theatrical force to be reckoned with both as an actor and a writer. By 1594 his plays were being performed by a tight-knit company of actors known as the Lord Chamberlain's Men. Five years later, Shakespeare and a number of his partners in the company forged a partnership to build a new theater along the south bank of the River Thames. They called their playhouse the Globe. In a career spanning approximately three decades, he produced no less than thirty-eight plays, 154 sonnets, and two lengthy narrative poems before retiring and dying at the age of fifty-two.

WORDS IN CONTEXT

sonnet
Closed-form poem consisting of fourteen lines and ending with a rhymed couplet.

New Life

For generations the origins, life, and mysteries of the Globe theater and its famous playwright appeared lost to history. Yet the least likely part of the Globe's history may have been its rebirth in the 1990s, when an enterprising American actor battled protests and financial problems to restore the playhouse to its former glory. Today, the work of archaeologists, scholars, and artists has revealed much about the Globe that had been hidden for so long and have therefore brought a fresh understanding to a vital form of artistic expression: "I regard the theatre as the greatest of all art forms," said twentieth century playwright Thornton Wilder, "the most immediate way in which a human being can share with another the sense of what it is to be a human being."[1] Without the Globe, much of that knowledge would remain unknown.

CHAPTER ONE

Theater Before the Globe

When the Globe opened in 1599, it joined nearly two dozen other playhouses looking to entertain London's masses. The Globe came of age as just one of many theatrical venues, but it quickly became the premier theater of its era, producing some of the best plays and actors in Elizabethan England. It continued a long theatrical tradition dating back to the ancient Greeks, the first purveyors of the performing arts. Since that earlier time, Europeans have staged plays in churches, inn yards, and public spaces where actors have told old and new stories in unique and innovative ways.

Miracle Plays and Merchant Guilds

Costumed performers in the Middle Ages were known as mummers. They could be found at country fairs and other places where crowds gathered. Mummers performed silently, miming activities and adding a sense of the occasion by pasting leaves to their clothes to represent the season or by wearing brightly colored outfits to draw an audience's attention. As the art of mummery evolved, practitioners began miming simple stories about love and courage and happiness.

In the 1300s another popular type of storytelling was the miracle play. Authored mostly by priests and performed by their local parishioners, the miracle plays were just what they claimed to be: acted-out versions of biblical miracles such as the raising of Lazarus from the tomb by Jesus. "The English drama, like the drama in other countries of Western Europe, began in the service of the Church," says historian Felix Schelling, "and at first was merely symbolic and a part of ceremonial [the church service]."[2]

Its purpose was to inspire religious devotion; entertainment, if present at all, was of secondary importance. Still, in a century when disease, death, and dreariness were facts of life, almost any kind of gathering and performance was welcome. Indeed, miracle plays drew hundreds of people who crammed local churches to see them, and in time the plays had to move outdoors to accommodate the crowds. Written in Latin, like most of the school books and other printed material of the time, miracle plays were pieced together by a variety of authors and staked no claim to originality. "No one of them can be regarded as a homogenous whole, the work of a single author," says nineteenth-century religious scholar Alfred William Pollard. "It is plain that the dramatists borrowed ideas and sometimes whole scenes from each other, and that the plays were frequently rewritten."[3]

The plays were typically performed on outdoor stages or platforms built by local workers. The players, too, were drawn from a town's population. In larger cities such as London, merchant and craft organizations took on the task of writing and performing the plays. These individual guilds, as they were known, took on discrete parts of the plays that fit their expertise. Carpenters, therefore, might present a scene in which Jesus is portrayed working with wood, since—according to the New Testament—carpentry was his trade as a young man. The baker's guild, conversely, might act out the Last Supper for their audiences. "The guilds were primarily economic units," say authors Thomas H. Greer and Gavin Lewis, "but they also performed personal and social functions. If a member fell sick, was put in jail, or got into some other kinds of trouble he could count on help from the guild brotherhood. The guilds provided proper ceremonies on the occasions of births, marriages, and funerals . . . and they celebrated Church festivals as a body."[4]

Guild Competition and the Moralities

What likely began as informal performances in time became more competitive. Before long these modest miracle plays became enormous theatrical events. Whereas costumes were simple at first, soon the guilds and other locals were designing and sewing elaborate gowns and creating lavish wigs and masks for the stage. In fact, the stage itself underwent a transformation when enterprising carpenters designed a large wagon upon which they placed their sets.

To give audiences a better view, the wagon's platform, or stage, was raised above eye level. Below the stage was a curtained-off area where performers changed costumes between scenes. The wagon sets, known as pageants, were wheeled and pulled from town to town by men or beasts. Along the way the pageant stopped, actors announced their presence, and, once a large enough crowd had gathered, the performance began. "They began first at the abbey gates," wrote local cleric Archdeacon Rogers in 1594, "and when the first pageant was played, it was wheeled to the high cross before the mayor, and so to every street. So every street had a pageant playing before it at one time, till all the pageants for the day appointed were played."[5]

Over the years the sets, like the costumes, became more elaborate. Craftsmen built sets portraying ships, castles, battlefields, and the like to add a greater sense of reality to the stories. One popular set, known as a hell-mouth, consisted of a demonic head opening its terrifying jaws. This horrifying portrayal of a devilish creature waiting to destroy sinners likely made quite an impression on medieval audiences.

In time the guilds and town councils financed the pageants; the church, therefore, exerted less and less control over public performances of plays. Consequently, by the early sixteenth century, plays were being performed in English, not Latin (the language of the church), and subject matter became more secular, suggesting experiences beyond religion. Pious works such as *The Story of the Creation of Eve* were replaced by morality plays, including the *Disobedient Child*

The arts, and especially theater, flourished in England during the reign of Queen Elizabeth I (pictured). Londoners clamored for stories and were willing to pay to see them acted out onstage.

or *Hickscorner*, whose characters—Pity, Perseverance, Imagination, Contemplation, and Freewill—model various personality traits. Biblical characters populated these plays as well, but they were typically employed to increase a play's humor or make a serious point about how one might live a better life. Success of the morality plays only increased throughout the mid-sixteenth century, as guilds funded larger and more complex performances for secular celebrations such as royal visits.

Amateur to Professional

As theatrical themes evolved, so too did the skills required to perform the plays. Morality plays were becoming longer and more complex, with more scenes, characters, and costume changes. In rare cases, the players were paid a few shillings, but this was not a wage a family could live on. Thus, when a festival ended and the pageant itself was stored in a local barn, the actors returned to baking or cobbling or other trades. But over the course of the sixteenth century, some ambitious amateurs formed their own acting companies, turning an avocation into what they hoped could be a profession.

Most of these people were more versatile and multitalented than their amateur counterparts. Apart from their acting skills, they might also juggle, sing, play an instrument, or all of these. And while the amateur players would act most of a play's characters, the professional might be brought on to portray a comic character in a portion of the play that became known as the interlude. The interlude—which usually included juggling, singing, and music—was separate from the main play. Thus, the budding professionals usually performed during breaks in the primary story and were known as the players of interludes. "The professional actors found themselves in a very isolated position," says theater scholar Karl Mantzius. "They stood in no connection with the

WORDS IN CONTEXT

interlude

A short dramatic piece of theater, usually introduced between the parts or acts of miracle and morality plays.

⬡ THESPIS AND GREEK THEATER

Little is known about Thespis, the innovative Greek performer who in 534 BC entertained Athenians and is credited with being the first actor. Aristotle, the legendary philosopher, suggests that Thespis did something no one had ever done before: He appeared on stage as a character and not himself. His stage was a handcart that Thespis pulled from place to place, looking for interested crowds. Once he found his audience, he would stand upon his modest platform and don handcrafted masks and costumes, pretending to be men and women, kings and slaves. After Thespis, people who took up his line of work became known as Thespians, or actors.

Greek performance evolved as each year a great festival was held in honor of Dionysus, god of wine. These grand theatrical spectacles were played out in open-air amphitheaters, shaped in half-circles with stone seats and flat, unadorned, ground-level stages. Playwrights such as Sophocles and Aeschylus competed at the festival by writing tragedies, plays that centered on a flawed hero whose doom was sealed by fate. Others wrote comedies that poked fun at human behavior. The actors, like Thespis before them, wore masks to signify their roles as kings, queens, beggars, and prophets. Thousands attended, seeing the plays not only as entertainment but as tributes to their many gods. Today only a small number of plays from that time survive. But they open a window into an ancient world that esteemed performance and storytelling as a reflection of the human condition.

serious subject of the play and the deep influence it exercised on the spectators; their business was only to divert the mind by their jokes."[6] The isolation of those who worked as professional actors no doubt contributed to a growing reputation that they lived immoral lives. Although no laws existed to bar them from theatrical performance, women did not take to the stage. As the fairer sex, they were considered too dainty, too good, and too honorable to associate with men of questionable reputation.

Age of Elizabeth

As a young noblewoman, Elizabeth, daughter of England's King Henry VIII, could ignore such standards and associate with whomever she pleased. In 1534 her father broke from the Catholic Church and established the Church of England. When Elizabeth ascended the throne in 1558 she quickly gained a reputation for being strong-willed, like her father. Her intensity was matched by a keen intellect and a deep-seated belief in the greatness of her country's destiny. She encouraged and funded the exploration of foreign lands, such as North America; supported a strong military to defend against and defeat England's foes, such as Spain; and quickly gained the admiration and respect of her compatriots.

In a time when kings and queens appeared removed from ordinary people, the red-haired queen worked to win their trust and loyalty by appearing more accessible. "Elizabeth had resolved to hold her subjects in awe with her majesty and delight them with her common touch,"[7] says historian Susan Ronald. This ability to connect with commoners extended and was likely encouraged by Elizabeth's interest in the arts, particularly theater. "Elizabeth was passionate about the theatre," writes historian Alison Weir. "The Queen also loved pageants, and sometimes took part in those staged in her Presence Chamber [a room for greeting guests], although she always appeared as herself, and it was not difficult to persuade her to join in the dancing that inevitably followed."[8] Holiday rituals and pageants remained the center of popular culture in the sixteenth century, but during the young queen's reign enterprising businessmen were also beginning to parlay these entertainments into profit.

Mass Entertainment

One of the more common forms of entertainment in the Elizabethan Age depended not on players, dancers, or musicians, but animals. When the queen hosted guests from abroad, bearbaiting was a common pastime. Before long this practice of leading a large brown bear into a ring and unleashing a small pack of dogs upon the growling animal became a popular and profitable form of mass entertainment. One Londoner of the time, John Stow, describes the excitement generated by this brutal but crowd-pleasing diversion: "For it was a sport alone of these beasts, to see the beare with his pinke eies leering after his enemies, the nimblenesse and wait of the dog to take his aduantage, and the force and experience of the beare again to auoid the assaults."[9] The high cost of acquiring bears to sacrifice to cheering, bloodthirsty crowds often required those putting on the show to replace them with horses, bulls, or horse-riding monkeys. The brutality of these animal shows was the chief attraction to a population whose own lives were far from easy.

The bubonic plague was an ever present threat to Elizabethans, especially in London. Approximately every ten years a new outbreak would kill thousands. Public events were banned once the death toll rose to forty. Despite these occasional epidemics, London grew in size and population at a rapid rate. In 1500 roughly fifty thousand people called the city home. A century later, that number had increased four-fold to two hundred thousand. Life expectancy was thirty-five years. Among the poor, one could not expect to live past the age of twenty-five.

London, at the time, was a walled city; its many gates—Aldgate, Bishopsgate, Newgate, Cripplegate—were locked tightly at dusk to ward off undesirables or attack. Narrow streets and the lack of regular sanitation kept the city cramped and foul-smelling. Still, opportunity kept people coming. It was where more of Queen Elizabeth's subjects wanted to be. "Few places in history can have been more deadly and more desirable at the same time as London in the 16th century,"[10] says author Bill Bryson. And in their free time, English men and women clamored for stories and were willing to pay to see players strut upon the stage.

Dawn of the Playhouses

London's population growth included professional players anxious to test their skills on the city's audiences. There, they also believed, they would find people like themselves and create acting companies in which

JACK OF ALL TRADES: PHILIP HENSLOWE

Without the diary Philip Henslowe kept from 1592 to1603, scholars would know far less about the day-to-day operations of Elizabethan theaters. Born in Sussex in 1550, Henslowe, when in his twenties, apprenticed to a dyer of fabrics. Upon the death of his master, Henslowe married the man's widow. Her husband's financial legacy enabled Henslowe to purchase inns, houses, and other property from which he made further profit. By 1587 he invested in the Rose and later helped finance the Swan in the west end of Bankside. Writers, though, eyed Henslowe warily: He often lent them small sums of money; in return, he demanded plays for his theaters. His business dealings also helped him acquire influential friends, and in 1592 Henslowe became a groom of the chamber, an honor bestowed on him at the royal court. The Globe's popularity and the Rose's diminished stature prompted the ever clever Henslowe to build a new playhouse north of the Thames, the Fortune.

Despite his theatrical investments, evidence suggests that profit, not love, kept him in the theater business. "Henslowe was a typical Elizabethan businessman and promoter," says author Marchette Chute, "and he was no more interested in the theater business than he was in the starch business or, later on, in bear-baiting." Despite his ambivalence about the theater, his cagey business sense inspired him to build the first "flex-space," an arena that could function as both a theater and as an animal ring.

Marchette Chute, *Shakespeare of London*. New York: E.P. Dutton, 1949, pp. 42–43.

to ply their craft. Yet this craft, at least as it was professionally applied, often harkened back to an earlier time. "Like the Drama," says Mantzius, "the earliest Elizabethan art of acting no doubt stood with one foot in the Middle Ages, without knowing where to put the other."[11]

Finding solid footing would take actors years, but exactly how they did it remains something of a mystery. Official records of professional theaters are scarce; perhaps theater itself was not deemed important enough to document. What is clear is that the phenomenon of building spaces designated for live theater performances was a new concept. By the time Elizabeth ascended the throne, local English inns were being used to stage play productions. London alone contained at least six inns where players performed. An inn's U-shaped, open-air yard provided ample room for actors and audiences alike. In the hours before a performance, an acting troupe built a rough-hewn stage at one end of an inn's courtyard. The performers used the inn's horse stables for dressing rooms.

As the hour of the performance approached, a member of the acting company stood at the inn's single entrance. With only one way in, theatergoers had no choice but to dig into their pockets and pony up the required gate fee. A percentage of these proceeds went to the inn's landlord. The building's balcony space was sold to wealthy audience members, most of whom came equipped with chairs. The less well-to-do entered the courtyard and stood during the performance. This actor-innkeeper financial partnership succeeded in drawing crowds, but a busy inn with its tavern also made for frequent interruptions during a performance.

First of Its Kind

Being forced to compete with loud and drunken audiences may have been what inspired entrepreneur John Brayne to open the Red Lion theater in the Whitechapel section of London in 1567. It was the first of its kind: a space dedicated solely for the presentation of plays. But what exactly went on at the Red Lion is lost to history because it had a short life, perhaps only two years. Yet nearly a decade later, Brayne tried again.

In 1576 he partnered with his brother-in-law, a carpenter and amateur actor named James Burbage, who imagined a circular space—an amphitheater—that would hold hundreds of people. London officials frowned on the idea. Theaters—like prisons, insane asylums, and factories for soapmaking and gluemaking—were considered too noisy, smelly, unsightly, and indecent to reside within the city walls. Despite this setback Burbage remained determined. After raising the money, he selected a building site outside London's gates in an area known as Shoreditch.

In only a few months time, Burbage and a team of workers completed their playhouse, which he dubbed simply The Theatre. It was, says historian Anne Terry White, "an inn-yard without the inn around it."[12] While no drawing or sketch of The Theatre has survived, experts believe it was open-air and roofless, much like a modern day sports stadium. Soon, The Theatre met with enough success to inspire a rival. Like many Londoners, Philip Henslowe made a living in any way he could. He was known locally as a moneylender, starch maker, and timber merchant, among other things, and challenged Brayne and Burbage by constructing the nearby Curtain theater. A few years later came the Rose, whose owners wisely built their playhouse near the city's Bear Garden to attract crowds with an interest in blood and mayhem. Bear Garden was a blood sport arena that featured fights between dogs and bears or bulls.

Puritans and the Queen

While London's theaters drew large crowds, their success was often muted by Puritans, a strict religious sect that denounced such entertainments as godless and sinful. Puritan leaders blamed a rare London earthquake in 1580 on the overabundance of theaters. Playhouses, they believed, drew unsavory audiences, presented unchristian behavior, and promoted prostitution in a part of town already known for its filth and poverty.

Another affront to Puritan sensibilities was the widespread use of cross-dressing in theatrical performances. The convention of the time, at least in England, was to have men play all the parts on stage. This, Puritans insisted, encouraged homosexuality, a capital offense in the Elizabethan era. "If you will learn to murder, flay, kill, pick, steal, rob and rove," wrote theater hater Philip Stubbes, "if you will learn to revel against princes, to commit treasons, to consume treasures, to practise idleness, to sing and talk of bawdy love . . . you need to go to no other school, for all these good examples many you see painted before your eyes in interludes and plays."[13]

Yet despite all of this outrage, playhouses had an important ally: Elizabeth I. The queen's love of theater was, by this time, well known.

Londoners seeking the thrill of blood and mayhem flocked to Bear Garden (pictured), an arena that featured fights between dogs and bears or bulls. Bear Garden's popularity helped attract attention to the nearby Rose playhouse.

But she also had a more practical reason for wanting to keep theaters open and crowds happy: Theaters, animal rings, and gambling parlors required licenses purchased from the government to stay in business. Those license fees earned hefty sums for the government's coffers. Plays, too, were heavily regulated and licensed.

The performance of each separate work cost the theater that produced it seven shillings and was paid to London's master of the revels. He, in turn, required the plays to be submitted to him for approval. After reading the work, the master determined whether it was appropriately respectful for London theatergoers. If the answer was no, playwrights and theater owners could be fined, arrested, or threatened with torture or dismemberment. In 1572 the British Parliament passed the Act for the Punishment of Vagabonds, which called for those without a license to be whipped. It also stipulated that actors could only perform with the consent and under the protection of a noble or royal patron.

Royal Patronage

London theaters thrived despite these legal threats. Indeed, the patron requirement provided theaters and actors not only protection but a reliable audience and financial support, especially when theaters were closed due to outbreaks of the plague. One of the earliest royal patrons was the Earl of Leicester. His support of a group of young actors enabled them not only to tour the countryside and earn a living during difficult times but to perform at a variety of London theaters.

Other troupes included the Earl of Pembroke's Men, who performed regularly at the Curtain theater and the James Burbage–led company named the Lord Chamberlain's Men. It was named for Lord Hunsdon, the lord chamberlain, an enthusiastic supporter of the arts. In the summer of 1594 Hunsdon devised a scheme wherein he and his son-in-law, Charles Howard, the lord high admiral, would establish like-minded but competing companies: the Lord Chamberlain's Men and the Lord Admiral's Men. The Lord Admiral's Men, to be led by noted thespian Edward Alleyn, were to be housed at the Rose in Southwark. Hunsdon, ever competitive and ambitious, coaxed some of the best actors from other companies—Lord Strange's Men, the Queen's Men, and Sussex's Men—to join his new company.

WORDS IN CONTEXT

master of the revels
An English court official from the late sixteenth century responsible for overseeing and paying for court entertainments such as plays.

Burbage's sons, Richard and Cuthbert, were also involved, although Cuthbert did not act. The company itself was a partnership in which each of the members shared the risk as well as the profit. Besides the Burbages, the Chamberlain's Men included actors John Heminges, Will Kempe, Augustine Phillips, Thomas Pope, George Bryan, Richard Cowley, and a relative newcomer from the small English hamlet of Stratford, William Shakespeare. In time Shakespeare's theatrical star would eclipse that of his fellow actors, but not for performing. Despite his acting skills, Shakespeare's work as a writer of plays would earn him immortality, and together these ambitious men would embark on a venture to build their own playhouse, the Globe.

CHAPTER TWO

Origins

A full understanding of the Globe theater and its place in the world is incomplete without acknowledging the man for whom the structure is now known: William Shakespeare. During his lifetime and affiliation with the Globe, no one gave a thought to naming it after the playwright. His contemporaries recognized his skill and popularity as a theatrical storyteller, but the Globe, when in business, was a partnership. Only in modern times has the Globe become synonymous with Shakespeare, considered by most scholars to be the greatest playwright who ever lived. How Shakespeare came to be involved with the Globe is a story that begins decades before the theater's construction.

Early Years

Shakespeare's father, John, was born sometime around 1530. His earliest years were spent on a farm in Snitterfield in central England, and he made his way to Stratford as a young man. There, 85 miles (136 km) from London, he took up trade as a whittawer, or a person who works with leather. Scholars disagree on John Shakespeare's ability to read. Legend suggests that like the majority of his fellow citizens he was illiterate, but he was a skilled craftsman, and most of them could read and write. In 1556 he was elected borough ale taster, which entailed observing the consistency of beer prices. By 1558 he had moved into the position of town constable, a kind of Elizabethan policeman, and one year later became an *affeeror*, a person who could assess fines.

Although the details are murky, John Shakespeare's reputation in the community likely attracted the attention of Mary Arden, the daughter of a wealthy landowner. The two married, and over time Mary bore eight children—four daughters and four sons—but a touch of mystery surrounds the birth of her third child, William, in 1564. Tradition suggests that he came into the world on April 23. The date annually marks St. George's Day, a national holiday in England. While there is no official record of his birth, other records indicate that he was baptized either on April 25 or 26. Infant mortality in the sixteenth century was high; babies were consequently baptized quickly, typically the first Sunday or religious holiday after being born. That year, April 23 fell on a Sunday. William might have been baptized two days later, the twenty-fifth, on St. Mark's Day, but no one quite knows.

Four years after William's birth, John continued his rise in Stratford politics when he was elected bailiff, the equivalent of town mayor, in 1568. At four, young William likely played with his two-year-old brother, Gilbert, in their large home on Henley Street. The Shakespeare house was located near the edge of town, although Stratford's main business district, Bridge Street, was less than a quarter of a mile away. Despite being a town bustling with taverns, shoemakers, and bake shops, the outskirts of Stratford consisted of farmland. According to scholar Stephen Greenblatt, Shakespeare was a country boy at heart:

> He had deep roots in the country. Virtually all of his close relatives were farmers, and in his childhood he clearly spent a great deal of time in their orchards and market gardens, in the surrounding fields and woods, and in tiny rural hamlets with their traditional seasonal festivals and folk customs. When he was growing up, he seems to have taken in everything about this rustic world, and he did not subsequently seek to repudiate it or pass himself off as something other than what he was.[14]

School, Marriage, and Departure

Historians generally agree that starting at the age of seven, Shakespeare attended the King's New School in the Guild Hall on Church Street not far from his home. The school, as stipulated in the Stratford charter, was free to local families and received funding through taxes. Latin, not English, was taught, written, and read in English schools, using a

Much is unknown about the early life of playwright William Shakespeare (pictured). Historians believe that he began appearing in plays soon after his arrival in London in 1585 and that he quickly made a name for himself as a comic actor.

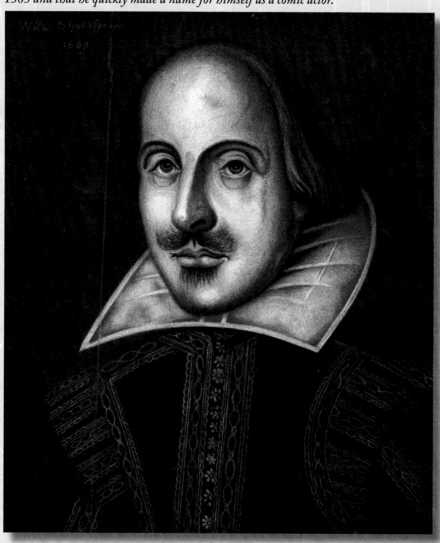

book written by Latin grammar scholar William Lily. "The whole of the English educational system united to pound Lily's Latin grammar into the heads of the young," says Shakespeare biographer Marchette Chute, "and if a schoolboy was wise he resigned himself to having to memorize the whole book."[15] Pupils endured long days, from six a.m. until sometime after 5 p.m., six days a week, sitting on hard wooden benches. Unruly behavior was punished with a whipping.

When William was twelve, an incident damaged his father's career and reputation. While the historical record remains unclear, John Shakespeare was accused of—perhaps even prosecuted for—wool trading and money lending, two serious offenses at that time. These charges caused John Shakespeare to withdraw from public life.

Three years later in 1579, William finished school and began his life as a young adult. In November 1582 Shakespeare married a local woman named Anne Hathaway. He was eighteen; she was twenty-six and pregnant. Little else is known about Shakespeare's bride, other than that she was one of seven children and that her father was well-off. Anne gave birth to their first child, Susanna, in May 1583. Two years later, in February 1585, they welcomed twins Judith and Hamnet. Beyond these facts, the couple's relationship is a mystery. "We have no indication of warmth between them," writes Bill Bryson, "but then we have no indication of warmth between William Shakespeare and any other human being. It is tempting to suppose that they had some sort of real bond for at least the first years of their marriage . . . [and] it may actually be that they were very loving indeed and enjoyed a continuing affection throughout their marriage."[16]

Like so much of Shakespeare's life, his journey from the small town of Stratford to the bustling streets of London and eventual fame is lost to history. London was a four-day walk or two-day ride from Stratford, but what exactly convinced Shakespeare to leave his family for an uncertain future in the country's largest metropolis remains largely unknown. Some scholars have guessed that he joined a traveling troupe of players after one of their actors, William Knell, was killed in a brawl with fellow actor John Towne. Knell's widow, Rebecca, soon married actor John Heminges, who would one day become one of Shakespeare's close friends and partners in the Globe theater. All that is certain is that in 1585 William Shakespeare packed up and set off for London and an uncertain future.

London Arrival

If Shakespeare had a desire to become a working actor or playwright and had friends with similar ambitions, he arrived in London at just the right time. The once nomadic troupes that eked out a living by

 ARCHRIVAL: CHRISTOPHER MARLOWE

Two months older than Shakespeare and the son of a shoemaker, playwright Christopher Marlowe earned respect by doing something Shakespeare never did: He attended college. In 1587, the same year Marlowe graduated from Cambridge University, his blank verse play *Tamburlaine the Great* made its debut in London. Performed by the Admiral's Men with Edward Alleyn in the starring role, the play succeeded in making Marlowe London's most famous new playwright. More plays followed, including *The Jew of Malta* and *Edward the Second*, yet the intrigue that surrounded Marlowe's real life was even more dramatic than his plays.

The English government regularly spied on its citizens, and in the spring of 1593 a wave of anti-immigrant posters bearing lines of dialogue from popular literary works of the day, including *Tamburlaine*, raised their suspicions. Officials interrogated dozens of intellectuals, including Marlowe's playwright friend Thomas Kyd. Under torture, Kyd accused Marlowe of personal cruelty and atheism, or denial of God's existence. Soon after, Marlowe himself stood before officials. They threatened to cut off his ears before setting him free. In May, Marlowe and three friends spent an afternoon drinking at a local inn. According to a later report, Marlowe and one of the men, Ingram Frizer, argued over the bill. Marlowe drew a dagger; they wrestled for control, and the blade landed in Marlowe's head. Scholars today argue over whether the death of Shakespeare's playwriting rival at the age of twenty-nine resulted from this violent argument or an assassination plot by the Crown.

performing in village after village now had chances to find permanent homes for their talents. Says Greenblatt, "The rise of the public theaters in a city with a rapidly expanding population hungry for amusement gave at least some of these companies the opportunity to have a lucrative home base where they would do most of their performing."[17]

Occasionally, these young players would again have to take to the road, but their once uncertain existence was gone. Historians believe that soon after his arrival in London Shakespeare began appearing as an actor in a variety of plays at numerous theaters. Some evidence suggests that he was especially talented as a comic actor, and three years after his arrival he was well known in London's theatrical circles. He would soon be asked to do more.

To turn a profit, theater owners had to fill their seats to capacity as often as possible. This meant encouraging more than two thousand people nearly every day to go to the theater. To do so, as many as five or six different plays would have to be mounted each week, a tremendous burden for writers and actors alike. The more popular shows would end up in repertory, a revolving schedule of plays, new and old, meant to keep audiences coming. No one knows whether Shakespeare counted himself as an actor first and playwright second, or the other way around, but the high demand for new material to perform must have been one of the factors that encouraged him to first put a goose-quill pen to paper.

Historians generally agree that his first produced play was likely *Henry VI, Part 1*, written about 1590. King Henry had ruled England more than a century earlier. Shakespeare's play, which may have been cowritten with fellow writer Thomas Nashe, tells the story of England's loss of territory and the buildup to the War of the Roses between the English and the French. By 1592 Shakespeare had completed parts two and three of the trilogy. In March the Lord Strange's Men theater company performed one play in the *Henry VI* trilogy—which one it was is in dispute—at Philip Henslowe's Rose.

First Recorded Mention

Poet Robert Greene may have attended one of those performances; in the summer of 1592 he mentioned the playwriting newcomer in his largely forgettable and long-titled pamphlet *Greene's Groats-worth of Wit, Bought with a Million of Repentance. Describing the folly of youth, the falsehood of make-shift flatterers, the misery of the negligent, and mischiefs of deceiving Courtesans. Written before his death and published at his dying request.* By that time Shakespeare may have already written as many as five plays, including *Henry VI*, although which of his other ones remains unclear.

As for Greene, his days were—as the title suggests—numbered. He had fallen ill after a night of drinking and carousing, but as his condition worsened he somehow managed to piece together his thoughts on his contemporaries, one of whom was Shakespeare. In his pamphlet, Greene, speaking to his fellow writers, paints Shakespeare as presumptuous and arrogant, a description that may suggest more about Greene's jealousy than the truth: "Yes, trust them not: for there is an upstart Crow, beautified with our feathers, that with his Tiger's heart wrapped in a Player's hide, supposes he is as well able to bombast out a blank verse as the best of you: and being an absolute *Johannes fac Totum*, is in his own conceit the only Shake-scene in a country."[18]

While Greene's reference to "Shake-scene" appears to be a direct and obvious reference to Shakespeare, the "Tiger's heart" comment parodies a line from Shakespeare's play *Henry VI, Part III*. Although more subtle, Greene's audience would have gotten the joke. "Johannes fac Totum," perhaps the unkindest cut, literally means "Johnny do-it-all," an allusion to a person with many abilities but who masters none of them—a mediocre talent. Greene did not live long enough to explain what young Shakespeare had done to anger him; he died on September 3, 1592. But Bryson harbors a guess. "Greene evidently felt that Shakespeare's position as a player qualified him to speak the lines but not create them. Writing was clearly best left to university graduates."[19]

Four days after Greene died Shakespeare again disappeared from the theatrical record, along with most of his colleagues, due to an outbreak of the plague. London officials ordered all theaters closed to help stop the spread of the disease, but death followed nonetheless. During the two years in which the theaters would remain mostly shut, more than fifteen thousand people succumbed to the plague. Meanwhile, actors and owners still had to make a living and were left with little choice but to take to the road, traveling again from town to town entertaining audiences great and small and living a meager existence.

Poet and Playwright

For a time, Shakespeare turned to poetry to earn his keep and support his family back in Stratford. While the writing of plays—like acting in them—was considered vaguely disreputable, composing verse and dedicating it to wealthy nobles was highly regarded and lucrative. In April 1593, just before turning twenty-nine years old, Shakespeare completed and published a 1,194-line narrative poem titled *Venus and Adonis*. He dedicated it to a young man whose patronage he hoped to gain, Henry Wriothesley, known also as the third Earl of Southampton and Baron of Titchfield. Early Shakespeare scholars suggested that Southampton paid Shakespeare £1,000 (£ is the symbol for *pounds Sterling*, the English currency), a sum far larger than Shakespeare had ever earned before. Others have dismissed the notion. Whether Shakespeare and Southampton maintained a friendship or ever met is unknown. Still, the poem became a huge hit with the public, the biggest of the writer's young career. During Shakespeare's lifetime, *Venus and Adonis* was reprinted more than ten times. A year later, Shakespeare published a longer poem, *The Rape of Lucrece*, and all the while he continued writing plays at a fast pace.

During the mid-to-late 1500s he wrote *Richard III*, *A Comedy of Errors*, *Titus Andronicus*, *The Taming of the Shrew*, and *Romeo and*

WORDS IN CONTEXT

patronage
The financial support provided to an artist by a wealthy noble, royal, or churchman.

Sometime in the mid-to-late 1500s, possibly during a period in which London's theaters were closed because of an outbreak of bubonic plague, Shakespeare wrote several plays. One of these was Romeo and Juliet, a tragedy of star-crossed lovers (depicted here in a scene from the play).

Juliet. Still, theaters in London were closed, so the only outlets for his works for the stage were traveling companies. He had been a member of Lord Strange's company and in 1594, after Strange's death, joined the Lord Chamberlain's Men.

That year the plague threat subsided, and London's theaters opened again for business. In June Lord Chamberlain's Men teamed with the Lord Admiral's Men to perform for ten days at a theater known as Newington Butts. There, under the management of Philip Henslowe, the two troupes worked together, sharing the same stage. Delighted audiences came to witness the acting skills of the two greatest actors of the day, Edward Alleyn and Richard Burbage. After their brief association, the Admiral's Men, along with Alleyn and Henslowe, moved to the Rose; the Lord Chamberlain's Men followed aging entrepreneur James Burbage to The Theatre, which lay across the river.

Partnership and Property

Shakespeare's affiliation with the company provided him acting roles, large and small, and at the same time gave the company access to his plays. One type of work fed the other: Shakespeare the actor stood upon the stage speaking the words of various playwrights as well as his own. In between rehearsals and the learning of lines, he scribbled his own stories. Although he had already written nearly ten plays, this artistic hothouse forced him to hone his craft. He shared his plays with his fellow players, who helped make them stageworthy by substituting new lines and reworking scenes until they were ready for public consumption.

The Chamberlain's Men also benefited greatly because having Shakespeare in their company ensured that all of his work would be performed exclusively by them at The Theatre. "When Shakespeare joined the Lord Chamberlain's," writes biographer Peter Ackroyd, "he brought with him all of his plays. This was their great advantage. From this time forward the Lord Chamberlain's Men were the sole producers of Shakespeare's drama. In the whole course of his career only they ever performed his plays."[20]

By 1598, despite its success, the acting troupe started by James Burbage years before was looking for a new home. Bickering between Burbage and landlord Giles Allen became heated. Allen wanted to tear down The Theatre and find what he considered a better use for the timber. The company purchased another property in an area known as Blackfriars, but locals did not want a theater in their neighborhood. Soon after, Cuthbert and Richard Burbage hatched a scheme to save their father's legacy and their livelihoods. A clause in their father's lease with Allen allowed the building to be dismantled and removed, but by now the lease had run out. The brothers wondered whether they still had the right to take The Theatre apart piece by piece. They both had something to lose. Cuthbert, as the current leaseholder, was most

ON STAGE: MEN ONLY

The Elizabethan stage was a men-only enterprise. While other European nations—Spain, France, Germany—permitted females to tread upon the stage, the English considered the life of an actor unseemly, impure, and inappropriate for women. In their place, young boys of ten or eleven were apprenticed to veteran players and given the female roles. Donning dresses and wigs, and painting themselves with white makeup, these beardless boys were the first to portray some of Shakespeare's greatest characters—Juliet, Desdemona, Portia, and Lady Macbeth. Once a young player's voice broke and he reached puberty, he often moved to male roles. Among the Lord Chamberlain's Men, the names of two boy players are most remembered: Alexander (Sander) Cooke, who apprenticed to John Heminges, and Nick Tooley, who spent two or three years in the home of Richard Burbage. Although the work was steady, the pay was poor, and the lead-based makeup used by the youthful actors was poisonous, leading to skin diseases and, sometimes, lead poisoning.

The practice of using men in place of women lasted until 1660. Ironically, some Elizabethans believed that men played women better than the women themselves could. "One argument for the use of boys for women in plays centers upon the preference for 'realism' expressed by Elizabethan documents," says historian James H. Forse. "Only boys, this argument holds, have the 'freshness' of face, and suppleness necessary for subtleties of feminine movement."

James H. Forse, *Art Imitates Business: Commercial and Political Influences in Elizabethan Theater.* Bowling Green, OH: Bowling Green State University Popular Press, 1993, p. 81.

at risk financially; Richard, meanwhile, had a company of actors depending on him for their livelihoods. If they did make a move, they decided, they could not tell Allen of their plans.

Moving Night

As the weather grew colder and winter approached, a possible solution slowly came into focus. One of their latest productions, Ben Jonson's *Every Man in His Humour*, had been so well-received that the Burbages were confident of receiving an invitation to perform at the royal court for Queen Elizabeth. Their confidence was well founded. On December 26 Richard Burbage and his fellow players performed Jonson's play at court. Then, on the night of December 28, the brothers, accompanied by their mother, a financial backer, and their friend Peter Streete, who was a carpenter and architect, walked to the empty theater and got to work. With them were more than a dozen laborers. This night, their beloved Theatre would begin its transformation. Their scheme, if found out, could have spelled disaster for the Burbage brothers. Their plan was to do the job quickly, so as not to raise Allen's suspicions, but the bitter cold made their work harder and slower.

The crew labored late into the night and far into early morning. Not all of the timbers could be salvaged, but the ones that could were carried down Bishopsgate Street in the walled city of London and down toward the frozen Thames River. History does not record exactly how the workers transported the pieces of wood. "It may be that the timbers were slid across," says scholar Peter Thomson. "It would have saved the toll on London Bridge, or the considerable cost of several trips in a Thames ferry."[21] However the wood reached the other side, its destination was certain. The Burbage brothers had come to terms for a piece of land a little more than 100 yards (91 m) from the Rose, Henslowe's popular playhouse.

By January nearly all of the salvaged wood, along with any new pieces of lumber needed to build the Bankside theater, had arrived. Allen, who was likely out of town during the nighttime deconstruction, was livid. His property was now little more than a vacant lot. An agreement on a new lease for their new playhouse was signed on February 21, 1599. The owner, London businessman Nicholas Brend, gave half the lease to Cuthbert and Richard Burbage, while the other half was assigned to five of the Lord Chamberlain's Men: Will Kempe, John Heminges, Augustine Phillips, Thomas Pope, and Shakespeare, all of whom now owned a 10 percent stake in the venture. This arrangement changed soon after the lease signing when Kempe left the troupe and sold his share to the other four, raising their individual financial stakes to 12.5 percent.

Construction and Completion

By the time of the secretive move, the building's master carpenter, Peter Streete, had already drawn up a detailed blueprint known as a plat. The initial design for their new Tudor-style playhouse was little different from The Theatre. The structure would give the impression of being round but in fact was a twenty-sided polygon. This design made for a stronger structure since the wood used would not have to be bent and, thus, weakened.

In the days immediately before construction began, Streete and his workers traced the shape of the theater along the ground so that they had a truer sense of its size and dimensions. Using geometry, they carefully calculated how to refashion the timber from The Theatre for this new, yet to be named, playhouse.

Once the weather warmed, the men vertically pounded piles—long, thick timber columns—into the soft-soiled marshland until they hit rock or solid ground. On top of this firm base, they built the playhouse's foundation out of red brick. Next came the frame: Heavy oak timbers known as ground sills were used to raise walls 30 to 35 feet (9.1 to 10.7 m) high. The three lev-

WORDS IN CONTEXT
plat
A detailed blueprint.

els, scholars estimate, had slightly different heights, with the bottom level measuring roughly 6 feet (1.8 m), the middle slightly less, and the third and final level providing the least amount of head space for audience members. The partial roof was made of thatch, or thick bundles of dried reeds. But, by design, it covered only the periphery of the theater.

After six months of hard labor, Streete and his workers had completed a gleaming new building. The venture marked a risk for all involved, especially the shareholders. If they could not draw an audience, accrued costs could put all six men into deep debt. But their past success gave them confidence that all would be well. For the first time in their nation's history, the playhouse would be a true actors' playhouse since they helped design, manage, and fund the place. "From a

The Globe Theater

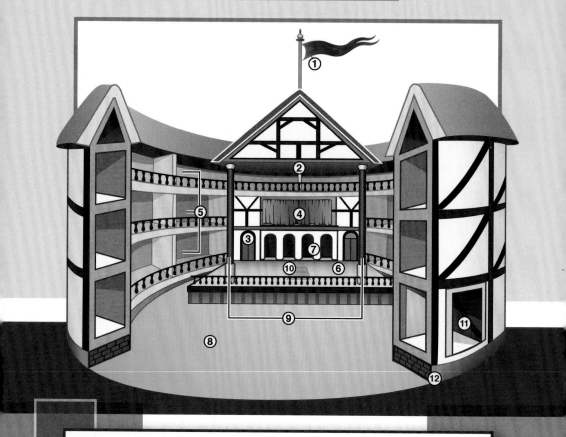

1) **Flag:** signified which type of play was being performed—black for tragedy, white for comedy, and red for history

2) **The Heavens:** ceiling over the stage that protected the actors from sun or rain

3) **Tiring House:** dressing and storage rooms

4) **Upper stage:** this chamber was used for most bedroom and balcony scenes

5) **Galleries:** three covered sections for seating

6) **Main stage:** for main action of the play

7) **Inner stage:** used mostly for indoor scenes

8) **Open yard:** audiences paid a penny to stand and watch the performances

9) **Support pillars:** wooden pillars that supported the Heavens

10) **Trap door:** actors playing ghosts or witches could descend through this door

11) **Theater entrance**

12) **Brick foundation**

dramatist's and actor's viewpoint," notes historian Glynne Wickham, it was "outstandingly the most attractive playhouse in London."[22]

For a name, these bold and ambitious men looked to a Latin phrase: "Totus mundus agit histrionem," or "The whole world plays the actor." Their work gave expression to all of humanity's joy and folly, triumph, and tragedy—it encompassed the world of man. Forever after, their playhouse would be known as the Globe. The partners reflected this idea on their new theater's sign, which portrayed Atlas bearing the world on his shoulders. The gleaming new Globe and its evocative sign announced to Londoners that a new playhouse was open for business and all were welcome.

CHAPTER THREE

Globe Heyday

Today, people worldwide have entertainment at their fingertips. Large-screen televisions equipped with TiVo recording equipment and state-of-the-art speakers bring a wide array of dramas, comedies, and reality shows into nearly everyone's home. If TV becomes a bore, consumers can immerse themselves in a World War II battle or a futuristic fantasy with a video game. Leisure activities in the sixteenth and seventeenth centuries were not virtual or passive. Instead, they required large-scale communal interaction often subject to the vagaries of weather and disease. For just a penny or two even the poorest Londoners could find hours of entertainment. In its day the Globe was one of the finest playhouses in London—a place where men, women, and children could be whisked to the canals of Venice, a magical island in the Mediterranean Sea, or the shores of the recently discovered New World. An afternoon at the Globe promised lords and ladies, scoundrels and damsels, a rowdy and rollicking time. In its heyday there was not a better place to be in the whole of London.

Opening and Controversy

The Globe opened on September 21, 1599, with a production of Shakespeare's *Julius Caesar*, a historical play of murder and politics. The date can be verified because Swiss tourist Thomas Platter, traveling with his half brother Felix, recorded the experience in his diary: "We witnessed an excellent performance of the tragedy of the first Emperor Julius Caesar."[23] Fifteen actors played to a nearly full house.

Almost from the beginning, the Globe theater was a stunning success. With Richard Burbage as its featured actor, and William Shakespeare as its playwright in residence, audiences flocked to watch a new play performed there nearly every day. Shakespeare's work had become quite popular, but one playwright could only write so many plays. Therefore, the Lord Chamberlain's Men produced the work of other contemporary playwrights, too, including Ben Jonson. The other London theaters, including the Swan, had no choice but to make room for a glimmering new rival. The nearby Bear Garden and its animal acts also bore the brunt of the Globe's financial success and saw attendance fall. And with a constantly changing variety of plays and some of the best actors London had to offer, the Globe kept audiences coming day after day.

In its first few years the Globe produced Shakespeare's *As You Like It*, *Othello*, *King Lear*, and *Richard II*. The latter, written by Shakespeare in 1595, stirred controversy when the Earl of Essex commissioned, or paid, the Chamberlain's Men forty shillings above their usual fee to produce the play at the Globe on February 7, 1601. Essex, a plotter against Elizabeth I, may have been trying to draw a comparison between the character of Richard II, a weak ruler, and Elizabeth and in this way incite a public revolt against the monarch. Eleven of Essex's supporters attended the play; the next day Essex attempted to overthrow the queen but was quickly arrested.

Elizabeth showed mercy to the Chamberlain's Men, who likely knew nothing about the plot. In fact, she invited them to perform the same play for her later that month, on February 24, the day before Essex's execution for treason.

Raise the Flag

In Elizabethan England, advertising was less sophisticated than today but no less effective. Historians estimate that 10 percent of London's population, or 150,000 people, attended a play every week. Each morning Bankside theaters circulated handbills throughout the city to announce which play was being performed that day. In the early afternoon the playhouses blew trumpets and hoisted a brightly colored silken flag high into the air on a flagpole to remind people—especially those living across the river in London—that the performance would soon begin. A red flag signified a history play; a white one comedy; and a black flag tragedy. "Each play-house advanceth his flag in the air," writes one Londoner of the time, "whither quickly at the waving thereof are summoned whole troops of men, women, and children."[24] Since the Globe and other theaters were open-air, the flags never flew on rainy days.

People had only two ways of crossing the river to reach the theaters: pay a few shillings to hire a waterman to ferry them across or walk across London Bridge, the only bridge that spanned the Thames. The city itself hardly resembled the sprawling metropolis of today. At the time, greater London—about 448 acres (181 ha)—extended only 2 miles (3.2 km) north to south and 3 miles (4.8 km) from east to west. Londoners, therefore, were used to walking. Their lives and livelihoods hovered around the Thames, which was nearly 1,000 feet (305 m) wide at certain points. Its depths contained a vast supply of sea life for fisherman to catch, including shrimp, flounder, eels, swordfish, and porpoises.

The bridge under which the mighty river flowed had been built in 1209. At 900 feet (374 m) long, the span brimmed with people and hundreds of shops. Business space on the bridge was highly valued, and in a time before skyscrapers, some of the buildings reached as high as six stories. A far more grim sight greeted theatergoers and other travelers on the Southwark end of London Bridge. There, officials displayed the heads of traitors and other criminals, stuck on poles. After crossing the bridge, playgoers had only a short walk to one of the theaters.

Arrival

Performances began daily at 2 p.m. Playgoers, however, often waited until the last minute to arrive. They entered the theater through a door in one of the building's towers. By request of its owners, carpenters had

London's theaters hoisted brightly colored silken flags high into the air to remind playgoers that performance time was near. A red flag (pictured in this illustration of the Globe) signaled a history play; white meant comedy and black meant tragedy.

framed the doors narrowly. This forced playgoers to enter slowly, one at a time. This ensured that patrons had to briefly stop to hand their admission fee—a penny—to the gatherers stationed there. At some theaters, those entering simply placed their money into a box, which, after the performance began, was taken to a nearby room for counting. This room came to be known in later decades as the box office.

Two types of patrons attended plays at the Globe: groundlings, whose penny admission fee gave them entrance to the open yard, and wealthy playgoers who paid for access to one of the three covered galleries that lined the theater. The first gallery, set below eye level to the actors on stage, provided what many patrons considered the best view of the action. Despite the extra cost, seating in the first gallery was typically filled to capacity. Some playgoers preferred the other levels to the first. According to scholar Andrew Gurr, the first gallery was, in fact, the worst one from which to see a play: "It not only meant watching the action from behind the groundlings but had the worst acoustics of the three levels, behind the shuffling groundlings and lacking the elevation of the two upper galleries."[25]

The second gallery afforded its viewers a slightly higher angle from which to view the proceedings, and when that too was full, audience members had little choice but to climb the stairs one more level. Entrance to each of the three galleries was from the rear; general admission made the best seats available on a first come, first served basis. The seating itself was rows of benches, which afforded little comfort.

A Cut Above

For six to ten pennies more, those who desired more comfort and a closer view might walk along a corridor behind the first gallery to one of four compartments known as a "gentleman's room." Adjacent to the tiring-house, where actors changed costumes, and near to the stage door, were two such rooms. These private boxes were frequented mostly by affluent nobles who wanted to be seen wearing their finest clothing in public. These lords and ladies, princes and princesses, would then enter by the stage door and walk onto the stage before taking their seats. This way, these members of the leisure class could avoid contact with the lower classes while strutting the latest fashion across the stage for all of London to see.

Within this already exclusive portion of the theater were areas known as "lord's rooms." Situated above the doors of the tiring-house and overlooking the stage, the lord's rooms housed the most elite theatergoers who, if so inclined, could even play a hand of cards while enjoying the performance. Actors performed scenes in close proximity to those fortunate enough to be seated here. According to historian Tita Chico, theaters may have differed slightly

WILL KEMPE: COMIC ACTOR

Little is known about comic actor Will Kempe. Even his date of birth remains a mystery. He first came to prominence as a thespian in May 1585 when he was praised for his performance with Leicester's Men. After spending time abroad in Denmark and other European locales, Kempe's fame grew. He specialized in silly dances, clowning, and improvisation, in which an actor departs from the script and makes up his own lines, jokes, and pratfalls. Scholar Lene B. Petersen comments that he "is known to have exercised a high degree of 'stage independence,' evidently never submerging his own personality into his role." In other words, he usually played himself, not a character, and improvised his lines as much as possible.

By 1592 Kempe had joined Lord Strange's Men, who performed outside of London. Two years later he, along with Richard Burbage and Shakespeare, joined the Lord Chamberlain's Men. He helped create the roles of Dogberry in *Much Ado About Nothing* and the jovial Falstaff in two *Henry IV* plays, all by Shakespeare. Their Chamberlain's Men partnership lasted until February 1599 when Kempe abruptly broke with his fellow shareholders in the Globe for reasons that remain murky. He immediately sold his shares in the company and left, joking about his former friends and calling them "Shakerags." Two years later, his popularity waning, Kempe borrowed money from Philip Henslowe and joined another touring company, but he never repeated his past success. He died in poverty in 1603.

Lene B. Petersen, *Shakespeare's Errant Texts: Textual Form and Linguistic Style in Shakespearean 'Bad' Quartos and Co-Authored Plays*. Cambridge: Cambridge University Press, 2010, p. 125.

as to how their rooms for wealthy theatergoers were organized. "The Rose," says Chico, "even included a separate room for 'visitors of position' above the tiring-room. These privileged audience members were entitled to peer into the tiring-room. Going backstage was part of the price of their expensive tickets."[26] Wealthy viewers could even sit onstage, where as much as 10 feet (3 m) was set aside for this purpose.

Lively Place

The groundlings had the least comfortable of the theater's accommodations. Even though the raised stage forced them to crane their necks, little distracted them from the stage action. When it rained during a performance, they could seek shelter, for an added penny, in the first gallery. "In effect, the lower you were in the open-air playhouse," says Andrew Gurr, "the lower your social status. Artisans and craftsmen, apprentices, house servants and those of the unemployed who could afford it crammed into the yard, the rough-surfaced floor on which the stage platform stood."[27] There, these groundlings did little to curb their boisterous appetites.

Concessions were sold. People could buy apples and pears, which some later hurled toward the stage when unhappy with the play or the performers. Other treats included nuts, gingerbread, and the latest Elizabethan temptation: tobacco. The festivities were further enlivened by the sale and consumption of ale. By a play's midway point, the groundlings, especially, were loud and boisterous in their responses to the drama or comedy on stage. When they had to relieve themselves, Globe patrons had to improvise, since theaters had no toilets. Theatergoing was, thus, an experience that assaulted all of the senses.

The Play Begins

In the moments before a play began, audiences members were usually still milling around. Then, three trumpet blasts signaled that the play was about to begin. The first told the crowd that the players were ready; the second attempted to hush them; and the third occurred immediately before the play started. The actors entered through one of the tiring-house doors, where they had dressed.

Compared with theater and cinema today, the world as portrayed on stage was visually simple. Patrons saw little scenery, no curtains, and no attempt at an authentic portrayal of real life. Instead, playwrights used words to literally set the stage. Whether setting their scenes in a woman's bedroom, a castle tower, or on a wide battlefield, description alone created the scene. Shakespeare's history play *Henry V* (which takes place on the battlefield of Agincourt in France), uses a one-man chorus to set the scene and paint a visual picture for his audience. The words recited by the chorus include these: "O for a Muse of fire, that would ascend/The brightest heaven of invention,/A kingdom for a stage, princes to act/And monarchs to behold the swelling scene!/can this cockpit hold/The vasty fields of France? or may we cram/Within this wooden O the very casques/That did affright the air at Agincourt?"[28]

Ordinary props, or properties, and special effects enhanced the spectacle. Kings wore jeweled crowns and duels included swords. A pig's bladder well hidden inside an actor's coat spouted blood when stabbed, giving audiences a gory thrill. Other slimy animal innards might be displayed and splattered on the stage to suggest the aftermath of a battle. A wide trapdoor was raised and lowered using a simple hoist, or suspension mechanism, so that larger props such as cauldrons and beds could magically appear on stage. Another effective technique used was the hiding and revealing of characters from behind curtains. These hidden characters might be eavesdropping or trying to avoid capture. This simple but often powerful technique kept audiences guessing and only deepened a drama's suspense. The goal was to make the entire experience seamless for the audience, with little lag time between scenes.

The players also hoped to create a recognizable, if mostly symbolic, world for the crowds that filed into the Globe almost daily— a world in which evil was punished and good, in the end, prevailed. "The Elizabethan theater represents the stage as the earth," says theater scholar Tetsuo Anzai, "existing between 'heaven' (the ceiling above) and 'hell' (the pit below), the physical structure of the stage as a whole thus standing symbolically for the cosmos, the theater of the world."[29] Perhaps the most unsettling example of this was used in the play *Doctor Faustus* by Christopher Marlowe. During the play's most

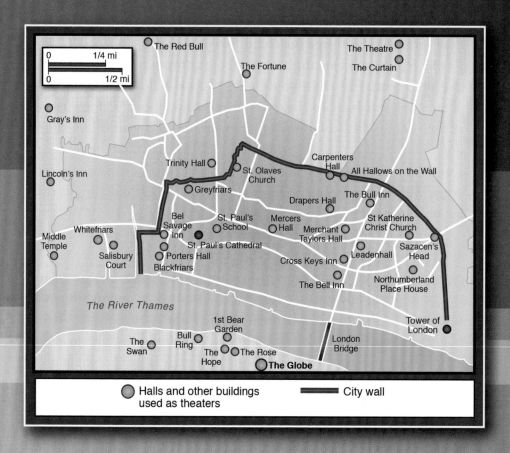

London Theaters c.1600

0   1/4 mi
0   1/2 mi

The Red Bull

The Theatre

The Fortune

The Curtain

Gray's Inn

Trinity Hall

Carpenters Hall

All Hallows on the Wall

Lincoln's Inn

St. Olaves Church

Greyfriars

Drapers Hall

The Bull Inn

Bel Savage Inn

St. Paul's School

Mercers Hall

St Katherine Christ Church

Middle Temple

Whitefriars

Merchant Taylors Hall

Sazacen's Head

Salisbury Court

St. Paul's Cathedral

Porters Hall

Cross Keys Inn

Leadenhall

Blackfriars

The Bell Inn

Northumberland Place House

The River Thames

Tower of London

1st Bear Garden

The Swan

Bull Ring

The Hope

The Rose

London Bridge

The Globe

⬤ Halls and other buildings used as theaters

━━━ City wall

dramatic moment, a golden throne descends from heaven, while a demonic-looking hell mouth spews smoke, suggesting the eternal fate that awaits the play's title character for making an agreement with the devil.

Backstage

Behind the scenes the Globe was no less dramatic. There, in the all-purpose tiring-house, actors changed costumes, donned wigs, and listened for entrance cues. To satisfy audiences that came almost all year round—even in the winter months—these players, when not performing, were preparing for the next play. That meant learning many lines in a short amount of time. Novices had the hardest time. They lacked the experience and hours of practice vital for presenting plays that could last as long as four hours. This meant a play might be full of flubs, misstated lines, or silent, empty moments when an actor forgot what he was supposed to say. Actors of the time coined a term for forgetting one's lines: "drying up."

To fight the mortifying feeling that came with dropping a line, players sometimes made up the missing dialogue on the spot. This in-the-moment improvisation was known as "thribbling," and playwrights hated it. They wanted their words spoken as written. To minimize thribbling, a play's meatiest roles were given to veteran actors like Richard Burbage or Will Kempe. But for a play like Shakespeare's tragedy *Hamlet*, even Burbage might have struggled. The title character, the gloomy prince of Denmark, speaks between fourteen hundred and fifteen hundred lines—nearly 40 percent of the play's total.

Little rehearsal time added additional pressure for all involved. Since plays were performed nearly every afternoon, this only left mornings and evenings to prepare plays that would go up the next week or even the

next day. No acting schools existed in Elizabethan England, so players learned their craft through trial and error. Younger actors relied on the advice and direction of older players to teach them how to perform with confidence and aplomb. "The preparation of the young player," says historian Ivor Brown, "meant a steady and strict training by his seniors in . . . the proper carriage of unusual costume, singing, instrumental music, stage-fighting, and of course, the most thoroughly, in speech and gesture."[30] The voice especially mattered when performing in an open-air theater with thousands of noisy and sometimes raucous people. Players had to project their voices and speak their lines crisply and clearly so that everyone could hear them.

As in most workplaces, the Globe was structured as a hierarchy. The shareholders, in this case the Lord Chamberlain's Men, were responsible for the entire operation. They were the initial investors and owned both the acting company and the playhouse itself. Because they shouldered the biggest risk, they reaped the largest share of the profits. But before they could take their profits they had to pay the hired men and boys. The hired men were mercenary actors not directly tied to the Chamberlain's Men. Plays often contained dozens of characters, far more than the core of six members. Thus, these actors-for-hire often filled out the other roles. They received little in the way of billing, which was reserved for the famous actors, and were paid far less than the shareholders. Beyond their work onstage, hired men also fulfilled most of the other positions required to run the playhouse, such as gatherer of money, stagehand, or tire-man, in charge of mending and preparing the costumes. The boys, meanwhile, were the apprentice actors who typically portrayed younger characters and female characters.

New Ruler

As the Globe and its performers flourished, England was experiencing a change in its own hierarchy. In 1603, after forty-four years and four months on the throne, Elizabeth I died. Never married and having borne no heir to the throne, she was succeeded by James VI, ruler of Scotland. His mother, Mary Queen of Scots, had been a longtime adversary of Elizabeth's. In 1587, feeling threatened by Mary's claim to the throne, the English queen had ordered Mary's execution. Now, years later, Mary's son claimed the English throne for himself; the new king became James I of England. Although his mother had been Catholic, James practiced Protestantism but tolerated Catholics in his kingdom.

Like his predecessor, he delighted in the theater, but James was a more distant ruler—nervous, sensitive, and altogether odd—in contrast to Elizabeth. Still, he and his subjects in London agreed on one thing. "The new ruler of England," says Marchette Chute, "had one characteristic in common with the thousands who flocked to

MACBETH: WRITTEN FOR A KING

Shakespeare's most chilling tragedy, *Macbeth*, is full of ghosts, witch-es, and bloody murder, yet its inspiration may have been the real king of England. In the summer of 1605 James I made his first official visit to Oxford University with his wife, Queen Anne, and son Henry. To entertain the royal visitors, Oxford officials planned and staged four plays. By all accounts the performances were disasters: The king fell asleep at one; the queen and her ladies-in-waiting took offense to a half naked actor during another; and the three royals did not even show up for the fourth play.

More successful was the welcoming ceremony designed by play-wright Matthew Gwinn. As the monarch and his family arrived at Oxford, three boy actors played out a pageant for them. Disguised as aged, toothless hags and carrying sticks, they sidled up to James and mentioned the name Banquo, one of the king's eleventh century Scottish relatives. They told him of Banquo's descendants, including James himself, who would rule forever. "Hail, whom Scotland serves," they shouted, "Hail, mighty Lord of Britain, Ireland, France." The brief play pleased and soothed James, a nervous man who needed re-assurance about his hold on power. It is likely that Shakespeare either witnessed the pageant or heard tell of it by someone who did attend. Less than a year later he and the King's Men performed his new play, *Macbeth*, at court. In it, three witches encourage a Scottish warrior to murder a king and steal his throne.

Quoted in Stephen Greenblatt, *Will in the World*. New York: W.W. Norton, 2004, p. 333.

the Globe playhouse each week. Neither he nor they could resist the plays of William Shakespeare."[31] The monarch's love of Shakespeare's work and of the Lord Chamberlain's Men in particular inspired him to become the acting company's new patron. Henceforth the troupe was known as the King's Men. Such notoriety only raised the group's profile and reputation further. During the winter of 1603–1604, it performed eight plays for the king and his family. A year later the royal court hosted the players eleven times. Seven of the plays were by Shakespeare, including *The Merry Wives of Windsor*, *Measure for*

Measure, Love's Labour's Lost, and *The Merchant of Venice*. The last title so enthralled the king that he asked the actors to perform it twice over three days.

Their responsibilities at court and at the Globe kept the King's Men extremely busy. Shakespeare himself had an exhausting list of duties, says Stephen Greenblatt: "He would have had to keep track of the receipts and expenditures; rewrite some of the scenes; help with the casting; decide on cuts [to the plays]; weigh in on interpretive decisions; consult on the properties, costumes, and music; and of course memorize his own parts."[32] Shakespeare and his partners were paid handsomely in compensation for the strains of writing, performing, and managing. Each performance at court earned the King's Men £10, a substantial payday. Each Globe partner not only received a large portion of these profits, but they also received a share of the Globe's rent, since they owned the building itself. They were, in other words, both tenants and landlords. Consequently, after but a few years of work, Shakespeare and his fellow owners were rich men.

By 1605 the Globe's future seemed limitless. The King's Men were widely considered the greatest acting troupe in London and the Globe the city's theatrical crown jewel. Yet Shakespeare's attention was pulled back to Stratford more than ever. Family joys and tragedy forced the playwright to reconsider his own future.

CHAPTER FOUR

Fire, Rebuilding, and Death

The Globe remained a London attraction for more than a decade, premiering the work of Shakespeare and other contemporary playwrights, such as Francis Beaumont, John Fletcher, and Thomas Middleton, and providing many afternoons of delight for thousands. Among the new offerings written by its chief playwright were tragedies such as *Macbeth*, *Hamlet*, and *King Lear*, as well as comedic romps, including *Much Ado About Nothing*, *Measure for Measure*, and *Twelfth Night*. The Globe also provided Londoners jobs as costumers, stagehands, accountants, and prop masters. Along with its competitors on Bankside, the theater was an essential part of the city's cultural life. Yet, as Shakespeare once wrote, "All that lives must die,"[33] and the Globe's life was cut short by tragedy less than fifteen years after it was built. A few years later its most famous co-owner would also succumb, yet in time his close friends would burnish his legend along with that of his playhouse.

Winter Playhouse

With their fortunes ever on the rise, the King's Men looked for new opportunities to make money. Playhouses, even under the best of circumstances, were subject to the ups and downs of city life and circumstances. Profits might be high one season and flat the next. Competitors—other theaters, bearbaiting rings—worked to draw ever bigger crowds. Acting companies worked to make as much money as possible wherever and whenever they could. Another consideration—the weather—also prompted London's most respected troupe to consider its options. The Globe, after all, was an open-air theater, and frigid London winters made playgoing and performing uncomfortable at the very least. Even with layers of clothing, actors and audience members alike often suffered from the weather during the colder months. A chance to expand the Globe's operations and provide a cozier venue for its audiences arose in 1608.

Twelve years earlier, James Burbage had purchased a large chamber in an abandoned friary. The space was located within the city walls and was thus easily accessible to audiences. He quickly converted the space to an indoor playhouse and called his new theater Blackfriars, after the black-robed Friars Preachers (Dominicans) who once inhabited it. But despite Burbage's hard work, dedication, and enthusiasm, the project barely got off the ground. Local citizens feared that Burbage and his troupe, then known as the Lord Chamberlain's Men, would attract lewd and uncivilized vagrants. They protested the opening of a theater in their neighborhood by signing a petition against Blackfriars. The petition was so successful that the acting company's patron, the lord chamberlain himself, signed it. After Burbage died in 1597, his sons Richard and Cuthbert took ownership of the dormant Blackfriars.

By 1608 the locals were only slightly less resistant to the idea of a public playhouse in their midst, but the successful and renowned King's Men decided to lease the Blackfriars from the Burbage brothers nonetheless. They did so on August 9 in the midst of another outbreak of plague, which was killing at least 50 Londoners per week.

WORDS IN CONTEXT

friary

A place of residence occupied by friars, living together under religious vows.

The Globe's open-air design (pictured) exposed actors and theatergoers to the elements. This was a problem during the cold winter months.

One of the King's Men, shareholder William Sly, died from it on August 13. When the death toll increased to 147 a week in September, Sly's fellow company members postponed the opening of the Blackfriars indefinitely.

Historical records indicate that between July 1608 and February 1610, only a few plays were performed in the city. The King's Men and other acting companies had little choice but to abandon their playhouses in favor of touring the English countryside or playing for their royal patrons. In April 1609 the King's Men earned a generous sum of £40 for duty to James I's court. A year later they added another £30 to their coffers. Documents show that the troupe was being compensated for "being restrained from public playing within the City of London in the time of infection during the space of six weeks in which time they practised privately for his Majesty's service."[34] This royal residency no doubt helped keep the King's Men financially afloat until the Globe reopened.

Poetry and a Grand Opening

In May, with preparations for the opening of Blackfriars well under way, Shakespeare looked to burnish his reputation as a man of letters. That month, London printer Thomas Thorpe published a collection of Shakespeare's sonnets. Written between 1595 and 1599, the 154 fourteen-line, rhymed poems on themes of mortality, the passage of time, love, and beauty presented a different side of the writer. Of the poems, 126 appears to address a young man, referred to in the sonnets as "fair youth." Two dozen others are written to a "dark lady." Like so many other aspects of Shakespeare's personal and professional lives, the exact identities of these people remain a mystery. As with the sonnets, plays written by Shakespeare around 1609 seemed most interested in romance. No doubt popular with audiences, plays such as *A Midsummer Night's Dream* and *The Tempest* present sprightly fairies, passionate young lovers, and intrigue. When Blackfriars opened in the winter of 1609, these plays could be presented in a more intimate and controlled setting. The indoor nature of the theater also allowed

ACTING LEGENDS

In the world of Elizabethan theater, Edward Alleyn and Richard Burbage had no rivals but one another. Little is known about how well they knew each other, but audiences knew them as the greatest actors of their day.

Alleyn, born in 1566, was the son of an innkeeper. He began acting as a teen, touring with the Earl of Worcester's Men. At age nineteen he was hired by a competing company, the Admiral's Men. Noted for his masterful portrayals, he earned the title of principal actor after only a few months. Alleyn's marriage to Joan Woodward, stepdaughter of impresario Philip Henslowe, brought him in contact with the business of theater. Before long he became partial owner and full-time manager of Henslowe's many playhouses. This lucrative career behind the scenes persuaded Alleyn to quit acting in 1598, but his many fans—including the queen—convinced him to briefly return to the stage. He died in 1626.

Burbage, born two years after Alleyn in 1568, had theater in his blood by way of his father, James. By twenty, young Burbage's fame was on the rise. He played many parts in plays by Marlowe, Jonson, and Kyd, but his close association with Shakespeare and the playwright's characters made Burbage a legendary figure. Unlike Alleyn, Burbage continued performing until his death in 1619.

the King's Men to charge slightly more per person; the higher admission price attracted a wealthier clientele; and the performances were lit by candles. This addition of artificial lighting and more sophisticated stage effects allowed the playwright to conjure an even more magical stage experience for his audiences than at the Globe. Thus, as 1610 approached, the shareholders now had two playhouses to run. Thereafter, each spring they returned to the Globe and performed through the summer and fall, but when the autumn chill turned to the freeze of winter they packed up their trunks and headed to Blackfriars.

Evidence suggests that King's Men dramatist Fletcher worked with Shakespeare on three plays over the next few years—*Henry VIII*, *Two Noble Kinsmen*, and *Cardenio*. By now Shakespeare was an elder statesman: honored and respected. For at least two decades his work had delighted Londoners and earned the accolades of critics and kings, but by 1611, Shakespeare had retired to Stratford. Little did he or his fellow shareholders know that in two short years their life's work would turn to ashes.

Fire

The summer of 1613 welcomed another season of theatergoing in London. Thousands made the daily pilgrimage to the local playhouses to enjoy the outdoor spectacle of enthralled lovers entwined, dueling rivals, and great armies in the moments before battle. One day in June—history does not record which day—Globe patrons gathered to hear a new play by Shakespeare called *Henry VIII*. As usual, the festivities were boisterous: Noisy groundlings milled about, sometimes echoing or commenting on the words spoken from the stage; vendors moved among the crowd, hawking their wares. Early into the performance, cannons fired and trumpets blared, heralding the arrival of the play's central character. Richard Burbage entered wearing his crown and regal robes as King Henry.

At first, no one noticed anything unusual, but sparks from the cannon rose into the air and caught on the thatched roof of the Globe. A patron seated high in the gallery watched as the sparks lit the dried grass of thatch and burst into flame. "Fire!" he yelled, causing the thousands in attendance to look up. The roof was ablaze, and the flames snaked down along the roofline and caught on the wooden walls of the theater. Chaos followed as the ladies and gentlemen of the galleries, the groundlings, and the players all dashed for the exits. One man's fancy breeches caught fire and, legend has it, he poured beer on himself to save his pants and his life. The audience members had escaped; no one was injured. The Globe, on the other hand, burned to the ground in less than an hour. Dejected Londoners mourned the loss of the Globe; many assumed it was gone forever. Local Puritan ministers, meanwhile, told their congregations that the fire and the Globe's destruction were signs from God. Theater, they told the people who filled their church pews, was sinful and against the laws of the Almighty. Shakespeare and his co-owners paid no heed to such remarks; instead they promised to rebuild.

Rebuilt and Renewed

Less than a year after the fire, the King's Men shareholders made good on their promise. Beginning with the charred but intact foundation walls, they quickly rebuilt the Globe, making it about the same size as the original. According to reports at the time, the new Globe was cleaner and somewhat fancier than the old version. To the theater's façade an ornate carving of the mythological hero Atlas carrying the world on his shoulders was added. Below this image, the shareholders added a line from Shakespeare's pastoral comedy *As You Like It*. Although printed in Latin, its English translation read, "All the world's a stage." The most important change was the new theater's fireproof tile roof, which virtually ensured that fire would no longer be a serious threat. These improvements cost the shareholders twice as much as had been spent on the first building, yet by this time, each of them was flush with cash from their theater business.

The new and improved playhouse opened in the summer of 1614; that June, Londoner John Chamberlain noted that those who attended plays at the new Globe rated it highly: "Indeed," he wrote, "I hear much speech of this new play-house, which is said to be the fairest that ever was in England."[35] Upon entering the new space, Chamberlain and his fellow theatergoers may have also noticed slightly more subtle changes. For instance, the stage was wider, stretching from the galleries on one side to the galleries at the other end of the yard. Storage space had also been added for actors and stagehands to store costumes and props.

This updated Globe also included more sophisticated machines for the creation of bigger and bolder special effects. Ropes, pulleys, and a 14-foot crane (4.3 m) used to fly actors and props in or out of the playing area were located in the tiring-house and hidden behind well-placed clouds or stars. These improved effects may have first been tried out and perfected within the controlled conditions of the Blackfriars. The remarkable improvements the King's Men made in their new playhouse had such an effect on audiences that a poet named John Taylor wrote a brief tribute to the theater and its owners:

As Gold is better that's in fire tried,
So the bankside Globe that late was burn'd:
For where before it had a thatched hide,
Now to a stately Theater is turn'd
Which is an Emblem, that great things are won
By those that dare through the greatest dangers run.[36]

Shakespeare Retires

By the time the old Globe burned, its chief playwright had already retired to Stratford, although the exact date of his departure from London remains unknown. Proof of Shakespeare's occasional return to London is virtually nonexistent, but it might be assumed that he traveled back to the Globe from time to time to oversee business matters and attend new plays at the two theaters he helped build. Shakespeare's final years in his hometown also remain mostly a mystery. Eighteenth-century poet and early Shakespeare biographer Nicholas Rowe wrote about the Bard's later life:

The latter Part of his Life was spent, as all Men of good Sense will wish theirs may be, in Ease, Retirement, and the Conversation of his Friends. He had the good Fortune to gather an Estate equal to his Occasion, and, in that, to his Wish; and is said to have spent some Years before his Death at his native *Stratford*. His pleasurable Wit, and good Nature, engag'd him in the Acquaintance, and entitled him to the Friendship of the Gentlemen of the Neighbourhood.[37]

Scholars suggest that by early 1616 Shakespeare may have been ill or decrepit. In March he signed his will bequeathing his estate to

Sprightly fairies dance in the forest in William Blake's illustration of a scene from Shakespeare's A Midsummer Night's Dream. *Blackfriars theater offered a more intimate and controlled setting for staging plays such as this one.*

his wife and children. He died on April 23, 1616, of unknown causes. One unproven theory suggests that Shakespeare died as the result of a fever after a long night of drinking with his friends, including playwright Ben Jonson. His burial took place two days later at Stratford's Holy Trinity Church. Family members placed a clever warning, perhaps written by Shakespeare himself, on his tomb:

> Good friend for Jesus sake forbeare,
> To dig the dust enclosed here.
> Blessed be the man that spares these stones,
> And cursed be he that moves my bones.[38]

Shakespeare was gone but not forgotten. His work continued to be performed at the Globe, and in less than a decade after his death two of his close friends and fellow shareholders, John Heminges and Henry Condell, made an effort to spread his plays far beyond their theater's walls. After years of work collecting his plays, in 1623 they produced and published *Mr. William Shakespeares Comedies, Histories, & Tragedies*, known today as the First Folio. By that time as many as eighteen of Shakespeare's plays had been published in single volumes, but this collection provided a more expansive and complete version of his many works.

Politics and Civil War

By the year of Shakespeare's death, the Blackfriars theater had replaced the Globe as the primary home of the King's Men. Its ticket prices—as much as six times higher than at the Globe—and more sophisticated and subtle performances drew wealthier audiences. But while Blackfriars profits far exceeded those at the Globe, the outdoor playhouse remained open and successful. Still, the class divisions seen at the two theaters were unmistakable: private theaters like the Blackfriars were exclusive; the Globe catered to all tastes but attracted a not-so-elite crowd.

Playwrights no doubt recognized the growing division and even animosity between the different economic classes and, in some cases, began using their art to directly comment on England's politics. The 1624 play *Game of Chesse* by Thomas Middleton criticized the foreign policy of King James, particularly the willingness of the king to negotiate with England's longtime enemy Spain. Audiences flocked to the play, which tweaked the widely held antipathy toward the Spanish. Although the play was a hit, earning huge profits for the surviving shareholders, London's Privy Council called a number of the company's actors in for questioning and put out a warrant for Middleton's arrest. Although the playwright somehow eluded authorities and likely fled, the King's Men were officially scolded and punished. By

⬡ SHAKESPEARE'S WORLD OF WORDS

The Elizabethan Age ushered in an explosion of language. The six-teenth century witnessed the introduction of more than 12,000 words between the years 1500 and 1600. At least half of these words are still used today. During his career, Shakespeare alone accounted for 2,035 words never before recorded in the English language. That is not to say he invented all of them, but before he used them in his plays and poetry they were unknown in print. These include now common words like "bump," "bold-faced," "employer," "howl," and "laughable," as well as slightly more obscure bits of diction such as "abstemious," "besmirch," and "pedant."

Scholars often stand in awe of Shakespeare's apparent linguistic genius; he was, after all, the son of a simple leatherworker from the rural hamlet of Stratford and probably had a less impressive vocabu-lary than the average person today. After an exhaustive study, English professor Marvin Spevack found that Shakespeare used 29,066 dif-ferent words in his plays and poems, although many are variations of other words. (Today, the average person knows roughly about 50,000 words.) Far more important than the number of words known to Shakespeare was his skill in using them. "What really characterizes his work," says Bill Bryson, "is a positive and palpable appreciation of the transfixing power of language."

Bill Bryson, *Shakespeare: The Illustrated and Updated Edition*. New York: Atlas, 2009, p. 146.

order of the king, the company could not perform again until further notice.

In a matter of months, the king relented, allowing his favorite theater troupe to once again ply their trade, but in only a matter of years politics and the theater became even more closely intertwined. In 1629, Charles I replaced James on the English throne. Far more than his predecessor, Charles sought to exert absolute control over his kingdom. Charles's controlling nature surfaced most blatantly in 1638 when he happened to read a new play called *The King and the Subject* by Phillip Messinger that was scheduled to be performed by the King's Men. So offended was Charles by the character of the king

William Shakespeare was buried in Stratford's Holy Trinity Church (pictured) in 1616. By the time of his death, Blackfriars theater had replaced the Globe as the primary home for the King's Men acting troupe.

as portrayed in the play and by what he considered the drama's insulting tone that he ordered the play suppressed. Censorship was likewise called for by the nation's Puritan ministers. For decades, Puritans had spoken out against what they deemed to be the unsavory nature of the theater, and by the early 1640s their voices had gotten louder.

An even more imminent threat loomed over not only England's theaters but the country itself. In 1642 the English Civil War began when King Charles I and Parliament, England's legislative body, clashed. The assembly, whose role it was to levy taxes and pass laws, was led by Oliver Cromwell, a dour and authoritarian Puritan.

In April 1642 the last recorded mention of the King's Men occurred when the company of actors was granted a license to perform the play *The Sisters*. By September of that year the Cromwell-led Parliament passed a strict law that resulted in the closing of London's theaters; all live performances and games were banned, including pastimes such as horse racing, bearbaiting, and cockfighting. Later, an ordinance barred any disturbance of "the Publique Peace, [that] are commonly accompanied with the Gaming, Drinking, Swearing, Quarrelling and other dissolute Practices, to the Dishonour of God."[39]

> **WORDS IN CONTEXT**
> antipathy
> *A strong feeling of aversion or dislike.*

London's Playhouses Fall Silent

The city's playhouses had thrived for more than half a century, but now actors, costumers, food vendors, and hundreds of others whose livelihoods depended on theaters were out of work. While courageous players attempted to continue performing despite the ban, they were soon forced to stop for fear of fines or whippings. Many players joined the king's army against Cromwell's Puritans; the Globe's musicians gained employment by playing for the marching armies. The playhouses, ravaged by weather and disuse, fell utterly silent.

In 1644, two years after the war commenced, the Globe fell victim to the axe and was torn down. Tenement houses to shelter London's poor were built on the site of the city's most famous theater.

The superior strength of Cromwell's army wore down the king's soldiers, and in 1649 the monarch was overthrown and beheaded. Cromwell worked to mold England in his severe image, and for eleven years the Puritans ruled the land. The death of Cromwell in 1598 led to the brief rise of his son, Richard, but he found little support in Parliament. The political upheaval that followed paved the way for the return of the dethroned king's son, Charles II, and a restoration of the monarchy in 1660. Like Elizabeth I and James I, Charles II loved the theater. He determined that new playhouses should rise from the London streets. But unlike earlier incarnations, the new theaters would be enclosed, much smaller, and cater to the elite and wealthy nobles of England.

The Restoration, as the period was called, brought the art of theater back to life in England. New plays were written, and the older ones of Shakespeare and his contemporaries were abandoned as young playwrights and performers forged their own, new path into the future. As for the long-dead and demolished Globe, it, too, disappeared into memory. The Globe remained but a footnote in the annals of theater history for the next three centuries.

CHAPTER FIVE

Globe for a Modern Age

Visionaries have often dreamed of bringing the past to life. In 1895 Victorian novelist and thinker H.G. Wells published *The Time Machine* in which he imagined a contraption designed to take its owner backward or forward across the millennia. Nobel Prize–winning novelist William Faulkner questioned whether time exists at all. He had a firm belief that it mattered little in the scope of human existence. "The past is never dead. It's not even past,"[40] he said. Faulkner's words are echoed in the many efforts to rebuild Shakespeare's Globe theater. From the late eighteenth century through the late twentieth century, academics, architects, and historians expressed fascination with the idea of resurrecting the Bard's theater. Yet despite the playwright's importance in the annals of world literature, several attempts to re-create his playhouse along the Thames failed. If not for the efforts of a bold American actor, that theatrical dream might never have come to pass.

Early Efforts

Since at least the late 1600s the stages on which actors trod were fully enclosed to keep out rain, snow, hail, and bright sun. The Globe, however, had a unique, open-air design, allowing plays to be performed in the daytime. But without blueprints or a model, the theater community and audiences could only imagine the one-of-a-kind conditions that a Globe-like structure would provide.

In 1790 scholar Edmond Malone gained access to the papers of Edward Alleyn. These contained vital information about Alleyn's father-in-law Philip Henslowe and Henslowe's career at the Rose and Fortune theaters. After studying Henslowe's diary and a 1616 engraving of London by Cornelius Visscher, which includes a view of the Globe, Malone imagined an octagonal building. Twenty-seven years later, in 1817, German academic and translator Ludwig Tieck visited London and immersed himself in Malone's work and Henslowe's papers. Tieck suggested using the specifications from the original builder's contract for the Fortune theater as a model for the new Globe. But rather than build the theater in England, he wanted it built in Dresden, Germany. Tieck enlisted noted architect Gottfried Semper. The plan failed because Tieck could not raise the money or enough interest. Semper's blueprint for the Globe-like structure would remain forever unrealized.

Still, the idea of re-creating London's famous theater did not die. The world of Shakespeare and the Elizabethans seemed so foreign and unknowable to people of the nineteenth century that the possibility of restoring this world excited the romantic ideals of thousands. Victorian England, especially, became enamored of the history and style of Elizabethan times. "The real drive to reconstruct his [Shakespeare's] theatre came more from a sense of its strangeness, its remoteness from the modern experience of urban life and theatre-going," says Andrew Gurr. "This introduced the urge to discover more about the peculiar circumstances that helped to generate those amazing plays."[41] To the British, this earlier epoch represented a nobler, gentler, preindustrial age where peace reigned. The Elizabethan Age represented the image of a more perfect England.

Despite a general enthusiasm for the era, the idea for a rebuilt Globe theater languished until the 1930s when Journalist F.C. Owlett, a longtime lover of Shakespeare's work, developed the idea of the Mermaid Shakespeare Society as a way of arousing interest in a Globe project. Owlett named the society after a legend suggesting that Shakespeare and Ben Jonson often retired to a tavern of that name after a hard day's work. Francis Beaumont, in a verse dedicated

⬡ A NATIONAL THEATER

Calls for a national theater in England began as far back as the mid-1800s. In 1847 a group calling themselves the Shakespeare Committee purchased the legendary playwright's birthplace in Stratford. Nearby, the committee hoped to start a theater. After many years, the committee's hard work paid off when the Shakespeare Memorial Theatre opened in Stratford in April 1879. Its resident company of actors was dubbed the New Shakespeare Company and is now known as the Royal Shakespeare Company.

In 1902 the London Shakespeare League was formed to address the absence of quality theater productions in London, but two world wars put the project on hold. Finally in 1948, a site was chosen, and Parliament passed the National Theatre Act, which provided financial support. Fourteen more years of legal and financial problems followed, but in October 1963 the Royal National Theatre opened its doors and welcomed audiences to a production of *Hamlet*. From its opening until 1976, the company was housed at the Old Vic theater in Waterloo. Its first artistic director, noted stage and film actor Laurence Olivier, led the National through the early years. By 1977 the National had moved to its permanent home in the South Bank area of London. During its life, the National has produced hundreds of shows and drawn hundreds of thousands of people. Now led by artistic director Nicholas Hytner, the National recently began broadcasting many of its performances to cinemas in twenty-two countries, bringing its unique brand of theater to the entire world.

to Jonson, immortalized the story and the pub: "What things have we seen/Done at the Mermaid? Hard words that have been /So nimble, and so full of subtill flame . . ."[42]

Owlett delighted in the idea that this kind of wit, conversation, and merrymaking could be recovered in his time. He used his connections in the newspaper business to move the process of Globe resurrection forward. Joseph P. Kennedy, US ambassador to Great Britain and father to a famous line of statesmen, including a US president, joined the cause, as did a British royal named Lord Bessborough and three prominent Shakespearean scholars. All agreed that their design would be closely based on Visscher's picture in the 1616 engraving and include a tavern and a library. Then, before Owlett could secure financing for his project, the local government chose the proposed spot for the new Globe for a new power station instead. The project fizzled in 1939 when Great Britain went to war with Nazi Germany.

An American in London

In 1949, at the age of thirty, a Chicago-born actor named Sam Wanamaker traveled to London to shoot a film. There he came up with an idea that would change London's landscape and reintroduce the world to theater as Shakespeare had known it. Wanamaker imagined the Globe rebuilt. "Rebuilding it in London has been the dream of many people over the years," he later said. "It became my dream when I first arrived in Southwark and found that the only record of Shakespeare's amazing twenty-five years of work in London was a bronze tablet."[43] Wanamaker took it on himself to remedy this oversight.

Wanamaker's acting career had ebbed and flowed over the years, but his quest to reconstruct Shakespeare's Globe along the Thames remained constant. "A reconstructed Globe, genuinely and carefully researched . . . will absorb the spirit of the original theatre," Wanamaker said. "People who come to it—whether in superficial curiosity, reverential love or deep appreciation—will experience something of the past."[44]

In 1969, after raising a modest sum to commence the project, Wanamaker turned to South African architect Theo Crosby. Crosby had earned a degree from the University of Witswatersrand in Johannesburg before immigrating to England. After working for a number of architectural firms, Crosby won a number of design awards and quickly gained a reputation for his brilliant designs. Wanamaker believed that Crosby had the vision and the persistence to help him bring the new Globe project to fruition. Crosby insisted on using natural materials, including oak and thatch, much like the kind used on the original Globe. "It was Crosby who gave Wanamaker's dream architectural expression, in which he insisted only on natural materials and high-quality craftsmanship,"[45] says journalist Peter Rawstorne.

But the dream remained in the planning stages, and before it could move forward, a significant amount of money would be needed. Consequently, in 1970 Wanamaker initiated the Globe Playhouse Trust as a way of raising funds for the project. His first patron was himself: He started with earnings from his television, film, and stage work. The trust was more than a hobby but less than a full-time job, and Wanamaker told himself that if he could not quickly find financial supporters for his project he would give it up. For two years he looked for but found no backers. Despite his promise to himself, he persisted. That same year Wanamaker found a promising location, a 1.2-acre piece of land (0.6 ha) that was used as a storage site for street maintenance machinery. The location, about 200 yards (183 m) from the original Globe site, was approved by the Southwark council.

Actor Sam Wanamaker (left) rehearses the lines for a play. Through Wanamaker's determined efforts—lasting more than two decades—the renamed Shakespeare's Globe was rebuilt.

Two years later, in 1972, Wanamaker opened the Bear Gardens Museum on the site where the old bearbaiting pit once stood. He believed that the museum, which housed a selection of Elizabethan artifacts, might help promote his Globe project.

Wanamaker's Folly

Shortly after opening the museum Wanamaker began the long and painstaking process of finding a piece of land on which to build his dream. He first explored the possibility of reconstructing the Globe on the same parcel of land on which it first stood. That plan quickly fell apart; the original site had long since been occupied by a historically valuable structure built in the eighteenth century. Years passed as Wanamaker juggled the demands of his acting career with the search for an alternate Globe site.

Each time he found what he deemed a suitable location, London authorities rejected his plan. The city, it seemed, was less interested in restoring one of its historical jewels than was a Chicago-born son of Russian immigrants. Newspapers soon caught wind of the actor's project and some commentators labeled it "Wanamaker's Folly," so convinced were they that a restored Globe would never come to fruition. These critics greatly underestimated Wanamaker's passion for the project, believing that he was simply looking to capitalize on their Elizabethan history and make fast money.

In 1982 Wanamaker convinced Prince Philip, husband of Queen Elizabeth II, to support and promote the new Globe. That same year Wanamaker gained the scholarly help of John Orrell, who came upon evidence about the shape and dimensions of the original Globe's exterior sketched by an English artist named Wenceslas Hollar in the late 1630s or early 1640s. Known by scholars today as the "Long View," it shows the city from an unusual position: just above and behind the tower of Southwark Cathedral. In Shakespeare's time the cathedral was known as the Church of St. Saviour and St. Mary Overie. The vantage point was an impossible one because no building existed that looked down from just this angle at the cathedral. "So it is a view," says Bill Bryson, "entirely accurate as far as can be made out— that no human had ever seen."[46]

Somehow through the powers of imagination, Hollar had drafted a fine and detailed panorama that showed the second Globe from roughly 900 feet (274 m) away. A close study provided the designers of the new Globe with an invaluable resource for reconstructing the theater along the banks of the Thames.

Wanamaker's Victory

Despite this promise of royal support and the expertise of Orrell, skeptics remained. In 1984 a London borough council tried to shut down the Globe project, arguing that Wanamaker's concept was just a get-rich-quick scheme. They suggested that a rebuilt Globe would be little more than a Shakespearean Disneyland, expensive and shallow. Others doubted the wisdom of building an open-air theater in a city where fog, clouds, and rain were nearly constant. No modern audiences, they insisted, would stand for hours, as the groundlings once had. Wanamaker believed that an open-air space could work, as it had so many years before. As for the critics on the London borough council, Wanamaker did his best to allay their doubts by enlisting the most respected Shakespearean scholars he could find to research what the Globe must have looked like and to ensure its authenticity.

> **WORDS IN CONTEXT**
> borough council
> *A governing body that oversees a community's bylaws, ordinances, and laws.*

Once he had a blueprint, he promised, the most skilled carpenters in the world would set upon the task of constructing the theater to its Elizabethan specifications. His ultimate goal, he said, was not only to re-create this glory of long-ago London but to reach out to ordinary people and provide them a theatrical experience like no other. "In all my professional life," said Wanamaker, "I've tried to do things which would have a direct relationship with 'the people', based on the premise that theatre can be a great force for social change."[47]

The local court battle with the borough council over his plans raged for two years until a high court finally sided with Wanamaker. In 1987 the new site was finally cleared of debris and prepared for construction. Excavation on the site began that same year, as did work on the diaphragm wall, which, if successful, would keep water from the Thames from flooding the site. One year later, after so much work, the project went broke; Wanamaker and his supporters again were forced to delay their dream.

Discovery and New Life

An archaeological discovery in 1989 reinvigorated public interest in raising the Globe anew. That year archaeologists discovered the original brick foundation of the Globe on Bankside only 200 yards (183 m) from Wanamaker's proposed construction site. In an attempt to benefit from the press attention that this discovery received, Theo Crosby proposed what he called direct building. This meant that they would construct each part of the new Globe complex as money came in rather than wait to raise the full amount before starting work on the building. Breaking ground on the theater would highlight the project and encourage badly needed donations.

WORDS IN CONTEXT

diaphragm wall
Underground structural elements commonly used as retention systems and permanent foundation walls.

Crosby's idea worked. By the end of 1989 the Globe project gained a number of noted patrons, including acting legends Laurence Olivier, John Gielgud, Michael Caine, and Anthony Hopkins. Soon thereafter, philanthropists Armand Hammer and Gordon Getty also signed on, as did the Ford Motor Company. In only a matter of months, money was pouring in. With a significant portion of the needed $45 million now earmarked for the project, construction began in 1991.

First, the foundation was laid for the new theater complex. This slow and painstaking work lasted for two years, and in 1993 building

Wenceslas Hollar's "Long View" of London (pictured), dating to the 1630s or 1640s, provided a unique perspective of the Globe's exterior. The artist's work proved an invaluable resource for designers working on the theater's modern reconstruction.

of the theater itself began. Crosby's design echoed the natural building materials of the original structure. Workers utilized thirty-six thousand handmade bricks, 90 tons (81.6 metric tons) of lime putty for the Tudor brickwork, 180 tons (163 metric tons) of lime plaster for the exterior walls, and six thousand bundles of Norfolk water reed for the thatched roof. The Globe's pillars, which hold the roof in place, are 28 feet (8.5 m) high and weigh 3 tons (2.7 metric tons). Crosby's fellow architect on the project, Jon Greenfield, insisted that this attention to detail and authenticity would enable audiences to experience Shakespeare's plays more fully and as the playwright had intended them to be experienced. "One of our goals in reconstructing the Globe follows the concept of playing Bach on original period instruments," he says. "The listener finds out more about the music and how it was intended to sound. Seeing Shakespeare performed in the theater for which it was originally written will reveal even more about the text."[48]

WHO WROTE SHAKESPEARE'S PLAYS?

Despite the strong evidence that William Shakespeare authored the plays attributed to him, some scholars, historians, and amateur sleuths remain unconvinced. Delia Bacon, a playwright and short story writer, was one of the first doubters. In 1845 Bacon theorized that a group led by lawyer Sir Francis Bacon and Sir Walter Raleigh composed many, if not all, of the plays as a way of promoting particular political and social beliefs. Others studies soon followed, many of which argue that Shakespeare's limited education, humble origins, and brief life make his writing of so many plays unlikely. By the 1920s one of the more popular anti-Stratfordian theories, as they are often called, gave the credit for Shakespeare's plays to Edward de Vere, seventeenth Earl of Oxford. Members of the Shakespeare-Oxford Society of today see a connection between the themes and style of Oxford's many poems with that of some of Shakespeare's work, including *Hamlet*, about an eccentric royal who loves drama and sports. Still others wonder whether Christopher Marlowe, during his brief life, had found the time to write Shakespeare's plays as well. Contemporary movies, TV shows, and plays continue to toy with the question of authorship, yet a recent survey of historians suggests that only a small percentage believes it really matters. But for others, the question of who wrote Shakespeare's plays is echoed by American writer Mark Twain: "So far as anybody actually knows and can prove, Shakespeare of Stratford-on-Avon never wrote a play in his life."

Mark Twain, *The Complete Essays of Mark Twain.* New York: Da Capo, 2000, p. 418.

In 1993, with a portion of the complex completed, Shakespeare's Globe hosted its first performance: the Bremer Shakespeare Company production of *The Merry Wives of Windsor*. The company performed on a temporary stage dedicated to Sir John Gielgud, one of England's most respected actors.

Death and Life

As construction continued, Wanamaker's celebrity rose. After so many years of disappointment, Shakespeare's Globe was becoming a reality, and Wanamaker's efforts were being acknowledged. In early 1993 Queen Elizabeth II awarded Wanamaker the prestigious CBE, or Commander of the Most Excellent Order of the British Empire, for his sustained work to revive the Globe theater. But Wanamaker would not live to see the completion of his long-fought-for dream. Later that year, on December 18, Wanamaker died of prostate cancer. Less than a year later, on September 12, 1994, Crosby died at age sixty-seven during surgery for a lung infection.

By then the project had become a source of pride for British citizens, and Shakespeare's Globe welcomed them for tours in the fall of 1994. Although regular performances were still being organized, visitors could stand where the groundlings had once stood, or tour the newly built tiring-house. Completion was still two years away, but money was no longer a problem. In 1995 Great Britain's National Lottery donated £12.4 million to the Globe Trust to complete the foyer and visitor's center.

In early 1996, with construction mostly finished, British actor Mark Rylance was chosen as the new theater's first artistic director. That August, Rylance and a company of actors performed Shakespeare's *The Two Gentlemen of Verona* on the reconstructed Globe stage. As exciting as it was to perform there, Rylance envisioned the Globe as much more than a playhouse. "It is very exciting, that process of working with the academics and the builders," says Rylance. "They have got incredible devotion, incredible patience. The odd thing for me, and I guess for Sam before me, is to try to include lots of views and lots of people, and really my job [as artistic director] is to make the place accessible not only for the audience but also for the actors, also for the scholars."[49]

Opening

Queen Elizabeth II officially inaugurated the theater on June 12, 1997, with a production of *Henry V*. With a full slate of productions planned, Shakespeare's Globe quickly became one of London's most popular attractions. Like the original theater built so long before, the new venue attracted people from all different economic classes. "You had wealthy people buying a gentlemen's box for 300 pounds, bringing their own picnic and bottles of champagne, sitting up in the chairs having champagne during the play," says Rylance. "And below them for a fiver [a five-pound note] you had some kind of ragamuffin with dreadlocks, standing in the yard watching the play."[50]

For the actors performing on the stage, the experience was no less unique or revelatory. "It was like going to the moon, taking off your helmet and suddenly realizing there was no air," says actor Lennie James. "When the audience came in, all our rehearsal preparation seemed irrelevant. I have never performed in any play where the audience became so vocally and physically involved."[51] Yet one concern persisted. For years Sam Wanamaker had been accused of trying to build a tourist attraction, a Disneyland for theater lovers and the Shakespeare-obsessed. Those now in charge of steering his dream into the future dedicated themselves to creating an authentic working theater and providing tourists with a first-rate theater experience. To achieve this, they worked to follow the original Globe's blueprint and specifications yet also included twentieth century lighting and acoustics. In this way, they were creating a working, usable theater space in the image of Shakespeare's Globe rather than a dead, musty, museum replica.

WORDS IN CONTEXT

derelict

Abandoned, run-down, or neglected.

"We are wary of emulating the original Globe exactly," says development officer Rebecca Muir. "There's a danger it could become a museum, rather than a busy, working, modern theatre."[52]

On May 7, 2003, Sam Wanamaker's daughter, actress Zoe Wanamaker, accepted the Southwark Blue Plaque award, given to those who have made significant contributions to that area of London, on behalf of her father. A month later the plaque was unveiled outside the theater and placed there as a permanent reminder of the man who made the dream of so many a reality. In Zoe Wanamaker's estimation, her father's persistence and dedication had righted a cultural wrong. "Sam couldn't understand why on the South Bank, where Shake-

Shakespeare's Globe, as it looks today, is a testament to its namesake's genius and enduring appeal. Plays staged at the Globe continue to enrich and inspire performers and audiences alike.

speare wrote most of his plays, there was nothing there to celebrate it," she says. "The South Bank was derelict when Sam first had the idea that it could be opened up and become a cultural walkway. He couldn't understand why from the Festival Hall [east] there was nothing there."[53]

Legacy

That once barren plot of land now buzzes with the sounds of tourists. In the years before Wanamaker's death, Rylance became close friends with the project's founder, and he quickly came to share the man's vision. Rylance believes that somehow Wanamaker remains as a presence in the theater he helped bring to life. "I feel him very, very present," said Rylance in the months before the theater's official opening. "When a man commits himself to an idea, and it is so tragically not complete before he has to move on, I feel the soul and spirit of that man are present around it. . . . Sam's wry, smiling face, and his expletives, are present. He is an inspiration to me."[54]

Wanamaker's legacy will be keenly felt beginning in January 2014 when workers complete a new 340-seat, indoor theater space to be housed within the Globe complex. The theater will be named after Wanamaker, who first envisioned a smaller theater for the playing of more intimate dramas and comedies. The $12-million-dollar project will include two tiers of gallery seating and, like the Blackfriars of old, will be lit mostly with candles. "The Sam Wanamaker Theatre will allow the Globe to continue its experimental vision of going back to the future,"[55] says current artistic director Dominic Dromgoole. Like Wanamaker, Shakespeare's work—his compelling plots and mellifluous words that cut to the heart of the human condition—continues to inspire generations of young and old. "It is . . . an amazement to consider that one man could have produced such a sumptuous, wise, varied, thrilling, ever-delighting body of work," says Bryson, "but that is of course the hallmark of genius."[56] Today, Shakespeare's Globe stands as a testament to that genius and to all those actors, directors, scholars, students, and dreamers whose lives have been enriched as a result. The contemporary Globe provides today's audiences with an opportunity to peek into the past and catch a glimpse of a time that may not be so different from our own after all.

SOURCE NOTES

Introduction: Lost and Found

1. Thornton Wilder, *Playwrights at Work*. New York: Modern Library, 2000, p. 13.

Chapter One: Theater Before the Globe

2. Quoted in Felix Schelling, *Elizabethan Drama, 1558–1642*, vol. 1. Boston: Houghton Mifflin, 1908, p. xxiii.

3. Alfred William Pollard, *English Miracle Plays, Moralities, and Interludes*. London: Oxford Clarendon, 1898, pp. xxix-xxx.

4. Thomas H. Greer and Gavin Lewis, *A Brief History of the Western World*. Belmont, CA: Wadsworth, 2004, p. 243.

5. Quoted in Anonymous, *"Everyman" and Other Medieval Miracle and Morality Plays*. Lawrence, KS: Digireads.com, 2008, p. 8.

6. Karl Mantzius, *A History of Theatrical Art in Ancient and Modern Times*. London: Duckworth, 1904, p. 169.

7. Quoted in Susan Ronald, *Heretic Queen: Queen Elizabeth I and the Wars of Religion*. New York: Macmillan, 2012, p. 21.

8. Alison Weir, *The Life of Elizabeth I*. New York: Ballantine, 1999, p. 250.

9. Quoted in Richard L. Greaves, *Society and Religion in Elizabethan England*. Minneapolis: University of Minnesota Press, 1981, p. 444.

10. Quoted in Bill Bryson, *Shakespeare: The Illustrated and Updated Edition*. New York: Atlas, 2009, p. 68.

11. Mantzius, *A History of Theatrical Art in Ancient and Modern Times*, p. 168.

12. Anne Terry White, *Will Shakespeare and the Globe Theater*. New York: Random House, 1955, p. 35.

13. Quoted in Stefani Brusberg-Kiermeier and Jörg Helbig, *Shakespeare in the Media: From the Globe Theatre to the World Wide Web*. New York: Peter Lang, 2010, p. 17.

Chapter Two: Origins

14. Stephen Greenblatt, *Will in the World*. New York: W.W. Norton, 2004, p. 41.

15. Marchette Chute, *Shakespeare of London*. New York: E.P. Dutton, 1949, p. 15.

16. Bryson, *Shakespeare: The Illustrated and Updated Edition*, p. 64.

17. Greenblatt, *Will in the World*, p. 188.

18. Quoted in Marvin W. Hunt, *Looking for Hamlet*. New York: Macmillan, 2007, p. 45.

19. Bryson, *Shakespeare: The Illustrated and Updated Edition*, p. 114.

20. Peter Ackroyd, *Shakespeare: The Biography*. New York: Random House, 2005, p. 220.

21. Peter Thomson, *Shakespeare's Theatre*. New York: Routledge, 1992, p. 17.

22. Quoted in Thomson, *Shakespeare's Theatre*, p. 18.

Chapter Three: Globe Heyday

23. Quoted in Andrew Gurr, *William Shakespeare: The Extraordinary Life of the Most Successful Writer of All Time*. New York: HarperCollins, 1995, p. 103.

24. Quoted in John Cranford Adams, *The Globe Playhouse: Its Design and Equipment*. New York: Barnes & Noble, 1961, p. 379.

25. Andrew Gurr, *Staging in Shakespeare's Theatres*. Oxford: Oxford University Press, 2000, p. 34.

26. Tita Chico, *Designing Women: The Dressing Room in Eighteenth Century English Literature and Culture*. Lewisburg, PA: Bucknell University Press, 2005, p. 48.

27. Quoted in Gurr, *Staging in Shakespeare's Theatres*, p. 35.

28. William Shakespeare, *The Life of King Henry the Fifth*, ed. William Aldis Wright. Oxford: Clarendon, 1881, pp. 1–2.

29. Tetsuo Anzai, "Directing King Lear in Japanese Translation," in *Shakespeare and the Japanese Stage*. Cambridge: Cambridge University Press, 1999, p. 132.

30. Ivor Brown, *How Shakespeare Spent the Day*. New York: Hill & Wang, 1963, p. 119.

31. Chute, *Shakespeare of London*, p. 268.

32. Greenblatt, *Will in the World*, p. 365.

Chapter Four: Fire, Rebuilding, and Death

33. William Shakespeare, *Hamlet*, ed. Paul Moliken. Clayton, DE: Prestwick House, 2005, p. 22.

34. Thomson, *Shakespeare's Theatre*, p. 169.

35. Quoted in Jane Milling and Peter Thomson, eds., *The Cambridge History of British Theatre*. Cambridge: Cambridge University Press, 2004, p. 317.

36. Quoted in Charles Knight, "Globe Theatre," *The Penny Magazine of the Society for the Diffusion of Useful Knowledge*, February 16, 1832, p. 60.

37. Quoted in William Shakespeare, *Complete Dramatic Works and Miscellaneous Poems*. London: J.H. Bohte, 1823, p. iii.

38. Quoted in Laura Valentine, *Picturesque England*. London: Frederick Warne, 1891, p. 241.

39. Quoted in Benjamin H. Irvin, *Clothed in Robes of Sovereignty: The Continental Congress and the People Out of Doors*. Oxford: Oxford University Press, 2011, p. 31.

Chapter Five: Globe for a Modern Age

40. Quoted in Malcolm Cowley, "The Undying Past," in *The Portable Faulkner*. New York: Penguin, 2003, p. 595.

41. Quoted in Andrew Gurr, "Shakespeare's Globe: A History of Reconstructions and Some Reasons for Trying," in *Shakespeare's Globe Rebuilt*, ed. J.R. Mulryne and Margaret Shewring. Cambridge: Cambridge University Press, 1997, p. 28.

42. Quoted in Samuel Johnson, *The Works of the English Poets, from Chaucer to Cowper*, vol. 6. London: J. Johnson, 1810, p. 202.

43. Quoted in Philippe Planel and Peter G. Stone, *The Constructed Past: Experimental Archaeology, Education and the Public*. New York: Routledge, 2012, p. 109.

44. Quoted in Graham Holderness, *The Shakespeare Myth*. Manchester, UK: Manchester University Press, 1988, p. 23.

45. Peter Rawstorne, "Obituary: Professor Theo Crosby," *Independent* (London), September 15, 1994. www.independent.co.uk.

46. Quoted in Bryson, *Shakespeare: The Illustrated and Updated Edition*, p. 98.

47. Quoted in Holderness, *The Shakespeare Myth*, p. 18.

48. Quoted in Richard Covington, "The Rebirth of Shakespeare's Globe," *Smithsonian*, November 1997.

49. Quoted in *Shakespeare: A Magazine for Teachers and Enthusiasts*, "The Opening of the Globe," vol. 1, no. 3, 1997. www.shakespearemag.com.

50. Quoted in *Shakespeare: A Magazine for Teachers and Enthusiasts*.

51. Quoted in Covington, "The Rebirth of Shakespeare's Globe."

52. Quoted in Claire Cohen, "Lifting the Curtain on Shakespeare's Globe Theatre," *Daily Telegraph* (London), August 24, 2012. www.telegraph.co.uk.

53. Quoted in Louise Jury, "Globe Theatre Appeal Stage Two," *London Evening Standard*, February 24, 2012. www.standard.co.uk.

54. Quoted in Ray Moseley, "Sam Wanamaker's Dream Finally May Come to Life," *Chicago Tribune*, October 22, 1995. http://articles.chicagotribune.com.

55. Quoted in Patrick Healy, "Shakespeare's Globe Sets 2014 Opening Date for Indoor Theater," *Artsbeat* (blog), NYTimes.com, November 27, 2012. http://artsbeat.blogs.nytimes.com.

56. Quoted in Bryson, *Shakespeare: The Illustrated and Updated Edition*, p. 247.

FACTS ABOUT SHAKESPEARE'S GLOBE THEATER

Ownership

- The original Globe was jointly owned by six members of the Lord Chamberlain's Men.
- At Christmas 1598, the Globe's owners took out a thirty-one-year lease on the property.
- As a shareholder in the Globe, William Shakespeare owned 12.5 percent of the theater.

Construction

- The theater was built in six months and opened for performances in September 1599.
- The timber for the Globe theater was actually reused wood from The Theatre—an earlier theater owned by James Burbage.
- The Globe had three stories of seating and was able to hold up to three thousand spectators.
- Construction of the Globe cost between £400 and £600.
- The Globe's thatched roof was made from either bundled straw or reeds. Each tightly packed bundle had a circumference, or distance around, of between 24 and 27 inches (61 and 68.6 cm) and were between 3 and 7 feet (0.9 and 2.1 m) long.
- It took American actor Sam Wanamaker twenty-seven years to raise the money to build Shakespeare's Globe.
- Shakespeare's Globe cost $45 million to build; apart from the theater itself, the complex contains a restaurant, shops, and a resource center.
- Builders spent $2 million sinking a diaphragm wall 1,000 feet (305 m) below ground to protect the new Globe from flooding by the nearby River Thames.

Measurements
- The original Globe's diameter—the distance from one side to another—was 100 feet (30.5 m).
- The walls of the Globe were between 30 and 35 feet (9.1 and 10.7 m) high—its height was, therefore, roughly one-third of its width.
- Actors performing at the Globe stood on a stage between 43 and 44 feet (13.1 and 13.4 m) across and almost thirty feet (9.1 m) deep, or front to back.
- The stage stood nearly 6 feet (1.8 m) above the yard floor.
- Shakespeare's Globe, completed in 1997, sits 200 yards (183 m) from the original site.

Attendance
- As many as three thousand people could squeeze into the Globe at one time.
- Outbreaks of the plague forced the closure of London theaters in 1593, 1603, and 1608.
- Approximately 150,000 Londoners attended playhouses per week— 10 percent of the city's population.
- More than three hundred thousand people visit Shakespeare's Globe each year.

FOR FURTHER RESEARCH

Books

Jonathan Bate, *Soul of the Age: A Biography of the Mind of William Shakespeare*. New York: Random House, 2009.

Bill Bryson, *Shakespeare*. New York: HarperCollins, 2009.

Christie Carson and Farah Karim-Coopers, eds., *Shakespeare's Globe: A Theatrical Experiment*. London: Cambridge University, 2008.

Stuart A. Kallen, *Elizabethan England*. San Diego, CA: Reference-Point, 2013.

Reginald Nelson, *How to Start Your Own Theatre Company*. Chicago: Chicago Review, 2010.

William Shakespeare, *The Arden Shakespeare Complete Works*. Edited by G.R. Proudfoot, Ann Thompson, and David Scott Kastan. London: Methuen, 2011.

A.N. Wilson, *The Elizabethans*. New York: Farrar, Straus and Giroux, 2012.

Websites

Folger Shakespeare Library (www.folger.edu). The Folger, located in Washington, DC, contains the largest collection of printed works by the Bard, as well as other materials from the early modern period, 1500–1750. The library's website has, among other resources, a section devoted to students that contains Shakespeare study guides, games, and highlights from the Folger's collection.

Shakespeare Birthplace Trust (www.shakespeare.org.uk/home.html). For those interested in how it all began, this website provides an easy-to-navigate look at Shakespeare's birthplace in the English town of

Stratford-upon-Avon. Users can watch an introductory video, peer into the childhood home of Anne Hathaway, Shakespeare's wife, and read about the First Folio, the first collected edition of Shakespeare's plays, printed in 1623.

Shakespeare Online (www.shakespeare-online.com). Launched in 1999 by a freelance writer and recently named one of the top ten Internet sites for students, Shakespeare Online is a useful hodgepodge of information on the greatest playwright who ever lived. From script analysis to key dates to free access to the plays themselves, this site digs deep to answer intriguing questions such as what did Shakespeare look like? and why is *King Lear* important?

Shakespeare Oxford Society (www.shakespeare-oxford.com). Questions of authorship remain the focus of the Shakespeare Oxford Society, and the group's website attempts to sow the seeds of doubt succinctly and clearly. The Authorship FAQ provides a brief overview of its argument against Shakespeare and for the seventeenth Earl of Oxford, Edward de Vere. Browse their online bookstore to find a slew of anti-Stratfordian titles, and decide for yourself who wrote what.

Shakespeare Resource Center (www.bardweb.net/index.html). More streamlined and scholarly but no less useful, this site includes links to in-depth studies of Elizabethan England, the controversy over whether Shakespeare really wrote the plays attributed to him, and a generous reading list for the Bard-obsessed.

Shakespeare's Globe (www.shakespearesglobe.com). For perspective on the recently rebuilt Globe, check out this colorful site containing information on upcoming performances and ticket prices. If you cannot make it to London, take a virtual tour of the theater from the stage, yard, or gallery, or print out a poster from one of its past productions.

INDEX

Note: Boldface page numbers indicate illustrations.

Ackroyd, Peter, 34
Act for the Punishment of Vagabonds (1572), 23
acting companies
  formed, 16
  hired actors vs. members, 50
  playhouses as home bases for, 29–30
  plays performed per week, 30
  Puritans and, 22, 65
  See also specific companies
actors
  guild members, 13
  payments to, 16
  professional
    apprenticeships, 35, 49, 50
    learning lines, 49
    reputation of, 17, 35
    skills of, 16
    women as, 17, 35
advertising, 41–42
Aeschylus, 17
Allen, Giles, 34–36
Alleyn, Edward
  life of, 57
  Lord Admiral's Men and, 24, 29, 57
  at Newington Butts, 33–34
  at Rose, 34
Anne (queen of England), 51
antipathy, defined, 65
anti-Stratfordian theories of authorship, 76
Anzai, Tetsuo, 47
archaeology, 74
Arden, Mary (mother of Shakespeare), 26
As You Like It (Shakespeare), 41, 59
audiences, 10, 43–44

Bacon, Delia, 76

Bacon, Sir Francis, 76
Bankside theater district, 20, 41–42, 53
Banquo, 51
bearbaiting, 18–19, 53, 65, 72
Bear Garden, 22, 23, 41, 48
Bear Gardens Museum, 72
Beaumont, Francis, 53, 68–69
bequeath, defined, 62
Bessborough, Lord, 69–70
Blackfriars (playhouse)
  competing playhouses, 8–9
  design of, 56–57
  location of, 48
  opposition to, 34, 54
  as primary home of King's Men, 62
borough council, 73, 74
box office, 43
boys as actors, 35, 50
Brayne, John, 21
Bremer Shakespeare Company, 76
Brend, Nicholas, 36
Brown, Ivor, 49
Bryson, Bill
  on Greene's opinion of Shakespeare, 31
  on London, 19
  on "Long View," 72–73
  on Shakespeare's
    body of work, 80
    marriage, 28
    use of language, 63
bubonic plague, 19
Burbage, Cuthbert
  Blackfriars and, 54
  dismantling of The Theater, 34–35, 36
  Globe lease, 36
  Lord Chamberlain's Men and, 24
Burbage, James
  friary purchase by, 54
  Lord Chamberlain's Men and, 24
  playhouse in Shoreditch, 21–22
  Theater, The, 34

Burbage, Richard
  Blackfriars and, 54
  dismantling of The Theater, 35, 36
  as featured actor at Globe, 41
  Globe lease, 36
  life of, 57
  Lord Chamberlain's Men and, 24, 33,
    45
  performance for Elizabeth I, 35–36

Cardenio (Shakespeare and Fletcher),
  57
Catholic Church, break with, 18
censorship, 64
Chamberlain, John, 59
Charles I (king of England), 63–64, 65
Charles II (king of England), 66
Chico, Tita, 44–45
Chute, Marchette, 20, 28, 50–51
Comedy of Errors, A (Shakespeare), 32
Commander of the Most Excellent
  Order of the British Empire (CBE), 77
Condell, Henry, 62
Cooke, Alexander, 35
costumes, 14, 47
Cromwell, Oliver, 65
Cromwell, Richard, 65–66
Crosby, Theo, 70–71, 74, 75, 77
cross-dressing, 22, 35
Curtain (playhouse)
  competing playhouses, 8–9
  construction of, 22
  Earl of Pembroke's Men at, 24

derelict, defined, 78
de Vere, Edward, 76
De Witt, Johannes, 8
diaphragm wall, defined, 74
Dionysus, 17
direct building, 74
Disobedient Child (morality play), 15–16
Doctor Faustus (Marlowe), 47–48
Dromgoole, Dominic, 80
drying up, 49

Earl of Pembroke's Men, 24
Earl of Worcester's Men, 57
Elizabeth I (queen of England), 15

  death of, 50
  love of theater, 22–23
  performances for, 35–36, 41
  reign of, 10, 18
Elizabeth II (queen of England), 72, 77
English Civil War, 65
English language, 15, 63
Essex, Earl of, 41
Every Man in His Humour (Jonson),
  35–36

First Folio, 62
Fletcher, John, 53, 57, 58
flex-space, 20
Forse, James H., 35
Fortune (playhouse), 20
friary, defined, 54
Frizer, Ingram, 29

Gaedertz, Karl, 8
gallery seating, 43–44, 80
Game of Chesse (Middleton), 62
gentleman's room, 44
Gielgud, Sir John, 76
Globe, 9, 43
  after opening of Blackfriars, 57, 62
  capacity, 10
  construction of
    date of, 8
    materials used, 10, 36, 37
    shape, 9–10
  design of, 37, 38, 39, 55, 72
  destruction of, 65
  discovery of original foundation, 74
  fire and, 58–59
  location of, 10, 48
  London economy and, 53
  opening of, 40–41
  partners in, 36, 49–50, 52
  plays produced at, 53
  symbols on, 39, 59
  weather and, 54
Globe, rebuilding of
  after fire, 59–60
  early efforts after Restoration, 68
  Owlett and, 68–70
  by Wanamaker, 79
    construction of, 74–77

critics of, 72, 73, 74, 78
design of, 70–71, 72–73, 75
dream of, 70
first production in, 76
funds for, 71, 72, 74, 77
site for, 71–72
Globe Playhouse Trust, 71
Greece, ancient, 17
Greenblatt, Stephen, 26, 30, 52
Greene, Robert, 31
Greene's Groats... (Greene), 31
Greenfield, Jon, 75
Greer, Thomas H., 13–14
groundlings, 43, 44, 46
guilds, 13–14, 16
Gurr, Andrew, 44, 46, 68
Gwinn, Michael, 51

Hamlet (Shakespeare), 49, 69
handbills, 41–42
Hathaway, Anne, 28
hell-mouth set, 14
Heminges, John
   Globe lease, 36
   publication of Shakespeare's plays, 62
   relationship with Shakespeare, 28–29
Henry IV (Shakespeare), 45
Henry V (Shakespeare), 47, 77
Henry VIII (king of England), 18
Henry VIII (Shakespeare), 57, 58
Henry VI trilogy (Shakespeare), 30
Henslowe, Philip, 20
   Curtain (playhouse), 22
   Kempe and, 45
   at Newington Butts, 33–34
   papers of, 68
   relationship with Alleyn, 57
Hickscorner (morality play), 16
Hollar, Wenceslas, 72–73, 75
Howard, Charles, 24
Hynter, Nicholas, 69

improvisation, 45, 49, 50
inns as playhouses, 21
interludes, 16

James, Lennie, 78
James I (king of England), 50–52, 56, 63

James VI (king of Scotland). *See* James I (king of England)
Johannes fac Totum, 31
Jonson, Ben, 35–36, 41, 61
Julius Caesar (Shakespeare), 40–41

Kempe, Will, 36, 45
Kennedy, Joseph P., 69–70
King and the Subject, The (Messinger), 63–64
King Lear (Shakespeare), 41
King's Men
   Blackfriars and, 56–57, 62
   last written mention of, 65
   partners' earnings, 52
   patronage of James I, 51–52, 56, 63
   production of *Game of Chesse*, 62–63
   purchase of Blackfriars by, 54, 56
Knell, William, 28
Kyd, Thomas, 29

Latin, 13, 15, 27–28
Leicester, Earl of, 24
Lewis, Gavin, 13–14
life expectancy, 19
Lily, William, 28
London
   description of, 19
   importance of playhouses in, 53
   population of, 19, 41
London Bridge, 42
London Shakespeare League, 69
"Long View" of Globe, 72–73, 75
Lord Admiral's Men
   Alleyn and, 24, 29, 57
   establishment of, 24
   at Newington Butts, 33–34
   production of *Tamburlaine the Great*, 29
Lord Chamberlain's Men
   Blackfriars and, 54
   building of Globe and, 10
   establishment of, 24
   Kempe and, 45
   at Newington Butts, 33–34
   responsibilities as shareholders, 49–50
   at The Theater, 34
   See also Globe; King's Men

Lord Hunsdon, 24
lord's rooms, 44–45, 46
Lord Strange's Men, 30, 33, 45
Love's Labour's Lost (Shakespeare), 52

Macbeth (Shakespeare), 51
Malone, Edmond, 68
Mantzius, Karl, 16–17, 20
Marlowe, Christopher
    as author of Shakespeare's plays, 76
    background of, 29
    death of, 29
    Doctor Faustus, 47–48
Mary Queen of Scots, 50
master of the revels, 23, 24
Measure for Measure (Shakespeare),
    51–52
Merchant of Venice, The (Shakespeare), 52
Merry Wives of Windsor, The
    (Shakespeare), 51, 76
Messinger, Phillip, 63–64
Middleton, Thomas, 53, 62
Midsummer Night's Dream, A
    (Shakespeare), 56, 61
miracle plays, 12–15
morality plays, 15–16
*Mr. William Shakespeares Comedies,
    Histories, & Tragedies* (1623), 62
Much Ado About Nothing (Shakespeare),
    45
Muir, Rebecca, 78
mummers, 12, 13

Nashe, Thomas, 30
National Theatre Act (1948), 69
Newington Butts (playhouse), 33–34
New Shakespeare Company, 69

Old Vic (playhouse), 69
Olivier, Laurence, 69
Orrell, John, 72
Othello (Shakespeare), 41
Owlett, F.C., 68–70

pageants, 14–16, 18
patronage
    companies formed, 24
    defined, 32

James I, 51–52, 56, 63
    rebuilding of Globe, 77
    of Wanamaker project, 71, 72, 74, 77
    Wriothesley, Earl of Southampton, 32
performances, frequency of, 48, 49
Petersen, Lene B., 45
Philip (prince of England), 72
Phillips, Augustine, 36
plague, 10, 19, 32, 54, 56
plat, defined, 37
Platter, Thomas, 40
players of interludes, 16
playhouses, 43
    Elizabeth I's support of, 22–23
    first, 21–22
    food and drink at, 46
    general design of, 43
    as home bases for acting companies,
        29–30
    in London area, 12, 48
    as new idea, 20–21
    physical structure of stage as symbol,
        47–48
    plague and, 10, 32, 56
    popularity of, 41
    Puritans and, 22, 65
    during Restoration, 66
    scenery and, 46–47
    seating at, 43–46
    special effects, 47
    transportation to, 42
plays
    actors' descriptions as scenery, 47
    licenses and approval required, 23
    See also specific plays
poetry, 32, 56
Pollard, Alfred William, 13
Pope, Thomas, 36
props, 47, 49
Protestant Church of England, 18, 50
Puritans
    burning of Globe as sign, 58–59
    censorship and, 64
    rule of, 65–66
    sinfulness of acting companies, 22

Raleigh, Sir Walter, 76
Rape of Lucrece, The (Shakespeare), 32

Rawstorne, Peter, 71
Red Lion (playhouse), 21
religion
    Catholic Church, 18
    miracle plays, 12–13
    pageants and, 14–15
    Protestant Church of England, 18, 50
    See also Puritans
repertory, defined, 30
Restoration, 66
Richard II (Shakespeare), 41
Richard III (Shakespeare), 32
Rogers, Archdeacon, 14
Romeo and Juliet (Shakespeare), 32–33, 33
Ronald, Susan, 18
Rose (playhouse)
    competing playhouses, 8–9, 20
    Henry VI performance at, 30
    location of, 22, 48
    Lord Chamberlain's Men, 24
    seating at, 45
Rowe, Nicholas, 60
Royal National Theatre, 69
royal patronage, 24
Rylance, Mark, 77, 78, 79–80

Sam Wanamaker Theatre, 80
scenery, 46–47
Schelling, Felix, 13
Semper, Gottfried, 68
Shakespeare, Hamnet (son of William), 28
Shakespeare, John (father of William), 25–26, 28
Shakespeare, Judith (daughter of William), 28
Shakespeare, Susanna (daughter of William), 28
Shakespeare, William, 27
    as actor, 24, 30, 34
    authorship issues, 76
    background of, 10
    birth of, 26
    body of work by, 80
    career of, 10
    childhood of, 26–27
    children of, 28
    death of, 61

    duties of, for King's Men, 52
    education of, 27–28
    English words first used by, 63
    Globe lease and, 36
    Greene's opinion of, 31
    marriage of, 28
    as playwright in residence, 41
    poetry by, 32, 56
    retirement of, 58, 60
    will of, 60–61
    See also specific plays
Shakespeare Committee, 69
Shakespeare Memorial Theatre (Stratford), 69
Sisters, The (play), 65
Sly, William, 56
sonnets
    defined, 10
    publication of, 56
    Venus and Adonis, 32
Sophocles, 17
Southampton, Earl of, 32
special effects, 47, 59
Spevack, Marvin, 63
Story of the Creation of Eve, The (play), 15
storytelling methods, 12–13
Stow, John, 19
Stratford, 64
    location of, 25, 27
    Shakespeare Memorial Theatre in, 69
    Shakespeare's life in, 26, 27
Streete, Peter, 36, 37
Stubbes, Philip, 22
Swan Theater, 8, 20
symbols
    of Globe, 39, 59
    of stage in playhouses, 47–48

Tamburlaine the Great (Marlowe), 29
Taming of the Shrew, The (Shakespeare), 32
Taylor, John, 60
Tempest, The (Shakespeare), 56
tenement houses, 65, 66
Terry White, Anne, 22
Thames River, 36, 42
theaters. *See* playhouses
Theatre, The (playhouse), 21–22, 34–35, 36

Thespis, 17
Thomson, Peter, 36
Thorpe, Thomas, 56
thribbling, 49, 50
Tieck, Ludwig, 68
tiring-house, 8, 44, 46, 48, 59
Titchfield, Baron of, 32
Titus Andronicus (Shakespeare), 32
Tooley, Nick, 35
Towne, John, 28
Twain, Mark, 76
Two Gentlemen of Verona, The
 (Shakespeare), 77
Two Noble Kinsmen (Shakespeare and
 Fletcher), 57

Venus and Adonis (Shakespeare), 32
Visscher, Cornelius, 68, 70

wagon sets, 14
Wanamaker, Sam, 71
 awarded CBE, 77
 Crosby and, 70–71
 death of, 77
 on importance of theater, 73
 legacy of, 79–80
 on rebuilding Globe, 70
 See also under Globe, rebuilding of
Wanamaker, Zoe, 78–79
weather, 54
Weir, Alison, 18
whittawer, 25, 26
Wickham, Glynne, 39
Wilder, Thornton, 11
women as actors, 17, 35
Woodward, Joan, 57
Wriothesley, Henry, 32

PICTURE CREDITS

ABOUT THE AUTHOR

David Robson's many books for young adults include *Colonial America*, *The Decade of the 2000s*, and *Encounters with Vampires*. He is also an award-winning playwright whose work has been performed across the country and abroad. Among his favorite plays by Shakespeare are *Hamlet*, *Macbeth*, and *Twelfth Night*. Robson lives with his family in Wilmington, Delaware.